PRAISE FOR *OZARK MOUNTAIN SPE*

"Brandon's *Ozark Mountain Spell Book* is full of amulets, charms, ~~and you~~
will be delighted from first to last."
—H. Byron Ballard, witch, farmer, and author of *Roots, Branches, and Spirits*

"Weston considers these magical operations and folkloric customs and understandings
as both a respectful researcher and a dedicated practitioner. Technical analyses of the
various components and combinations of spell work and talisman-craft are accompa-
nied by appreciations and explications of hillfolk cosmology, spiritual ecologies, and
magical ethics; artfully drawing attention to shifting historical influences upon Ozark
folk magic even as it collects and curates these rites and amulets."
—Dr. Alexander Cummins, author of *A Book of the Magi* and editor of
Revelore Press's Folk Necromancy in Transmission series

"Brandon invites you into his home, where he serves up history, folklore, and magic. A
wonderful and enchanting read."
—Katrink Karpetz, Witch of TheWitchery.ca

"The herbal knowledge ... that you will find within this book will give readers a fresh look
at how a deeply entrenched bioregional practice works magically with the local flora ...
We believe this information to be vitally important to share with others and find Brandon's perspective to be well researched, combining healing traditions from his elders as
well as his own praxis. This volume adds a new layer to the rich tapestry of Ozark magic."
—Catamara Rosarium, convenor of the Viridis Genii Symposium
and proprietor of Rosarium Blends

"This book is timely and important in that it helps give readers a broader grasp of the
subject of American folk magic with the clarity and authority of an author who has
dived headfirst into the subject of Ozark traditions."
—Marcus McCoy, editor and co-organizer of the
Viridis Genii Symposium and book series

"Not since the sainted Ozark folklorist, Vance Randolph, has there been such an important publication on Ozark folk magic. The fact that Brandon is also a gifted healer, from and of this tradition, offers us a curated collection of tried-and-true knowledge that is a benefit to us now and will be of benefit to future generations of practitioners and scholars."

—Rachel Reynolds, Ozark folklorist, head project steward
at Meadowcreek Community

"Weston's latest book opens up the world of Ozark folk magic to anyone interested, while still preserving the heart and flavor of this distinctive branch of North American folk practice. The spells themselves all have clear roots within tradition and history, but importantly provide variations that help them fit a modern worker's world. Weston explores depths seldom plumbed, such as the use of dream-based magical instruction, and connects the work to the words and actions of Ozarkers he's interviewed or found in existing folkloric accounts. This is a thorough course in mountain folk magic that invites a deeper understanding of a frequently overlooked region and demonstrates how fully integrated magic is within the Ozark worldview."

—Cory Thomas Hutcheson, author and co-host of *New World Witchery*

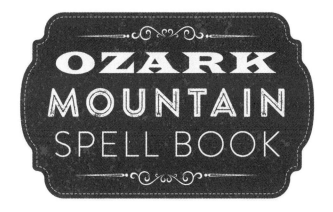

© Brandon Weston

ABOUT THE AUTHOR

Brandon Weston (Fayetteville, AR) is a healer, writer, and folklorist who owns and operates Ozark Healing Traditions, an online collective of articles, lectures, and workshops focusing on the Ozark Mountain region. As a practicing folk healer, his work with clients includes everything from spiritual cleanses to house blessings. He comes from a long line of Ozark hillfolk and is also a folk herbalist, yarb doctor, and power doctor.

OZARK
MOUNTAIN
SPELL BOOK

FOLK MAGIC & HEALING

BRANDON WESTON

Llewellyn Publications
Woodbury, Minnesota

FIRST EDITION
First Printing, 2022

Based on book design by Donna Burch-Brown
Cover design by Kevin R. Brown
Zodiac Man on page 18 © Mary Ann Zapalac, other interior art by the Llewellyn Art Department

Llewellyn Publications is a registered trademark of Llewellyn Worldwide Ltd.

Library of Congress Cataloging-in-Publication Data (Pending)
ISBN: 978-0-7387-7067-3

Llewellyn Worldwide Ltd. does not participate in, endorse, or have any authority or responsibility concerning private business transactions between our authors and the public.

All mail addressed to the author is forwarded, but the publisher cannot, unless specifically instructed by the author, give out an address or phone number.

Any internet references contained in this work are current at publication time, but the publisher cannot guarantee that a specific location will continue to be maintained. Please refer to the publisher's website for links to authors' websites and other sources.

Llewellyn Publications
A Division of Llewellyn Worldwide Ltd.
2143 Wooddale Drive
Woodbury, MN 55125-2989
www.llewellyn.com

Printed in the United States of America

OTHER BOOKS BY BRANDON WESTON

Ozark Folk Magic

To all Ozark healers and witches.
Past, present, and future.

DISCLAIMER

The old-fashioned remedies in this book are historical references used for teaching purposes only. The recipes are not for commercial use or profit. New herbal recipes should be taken in small amounts to allow the body to adjust.

Please note that the information in this book is not meant to diagnose, treat, prescribe, or substitute consultation with a licensed healthcare professional. This book is not intended to provide medical advice or to take the place of medical advice and treatment from your personal physician. Readers are advised to consult their doctors or other qualified healthcare professionals regarding the treatment of their medical problems. Neither the publisher nor the author take any responsibility for any possible consequences from any treatment, action, or application of medicine, supplement, herb, or preparation to any person reading or following the information in this book.

CONTENTS

Introduction

Let's begin with a story…

ONCE, MANY, MANY YEARS AGO, *there lived an old woman everyone in Nelson's Holler just called Gram Watson. She was a figurehead of the community, much beloved by everyone around, including more than a few suitors who vowed to remain chaste if they couldn't marry her. (Their hearts are still pining for the woman's affection even today.) Gram knew damn near everything about anything, and there was hardly a subject or task she couldn't just pick up and master almost immediately.*

Sissy Blackwell was once so famous for her homemade moon pies that folks came from all around Nelson's Holler to grab some at the biannual church revival. The reverend liked to joke that Sissy was single-handedly saving the community, one moon pie at a time. That was until Gram Watson learned how to make them.

One summer, Sissy Blackwell had spent all night Saturday and all morning Sunday making sure her batch of moon pies for the revival and potluck that afternoon was sheer perfection to behold. The chocolate on each pie was so smooth and evenly tempered it looked almost like a mirror, and she'd managed the hardest part, covering the sides with the chocolate too, with the ease of a seasoned professional. Reverend had even excused Sissy from attending church that morning, knowing full well she was still doing the Lord's work making those moon pies.

Sissy had never walked so tall and proud as she did carrying that platter of moon pies to the church potluck. She walked right over to the desserts table and went to set the platter down next to Miss Ida Lee's coconut cream pie, but then, with a jolt to her stomach, she spotted the treason. There, sitting almost radiantly in the afternoon sun, was another platter of moon pies and a little paper tag that read, "With love, Gram Watson." Sissy's faced boiled, but she managed to calm herself down with some words she repeated over and over in her mind: They're just moon pies. They're just moon pies. *And for a minute she felt better. That was until Reverend came over, the moon pie in hand revealing his treachery, and said, "Boy howdy, you sure got some competition!"*

Sissy packed up her moon pies, her faith, half of her friendships, and stormed back home that very afternoon.

It shouldn't have come as a surprise to the woman, though. Gram Watson had always been like that. Shoot, Sissy could remember when she was just a teenager and Gram Watson beat her daddy in the annual mule-driving contest without any known prior experience—either with driving or with mules. She saw the anger in her father's face as he stomped around the house throwing out swear after swear, saying Gram Watson had somehow used her magic to "witch" the competition. "You know she's got a book up in that house that tells her everything about everything?" he fumed to Sissy's mother as she sat calmly with her embroidery on the couch.

"Oh I know it, hun," she replied with a little smile.

The consensus around the community was that Gram Watson was a witch. That word wasn't thrown around lightly, though. It was wholly un-Christian to falsely accuse someone of any misdeed, especially being a witch. So, everyone around kept their opinions to themselves and chose instead to pass around useful euphemisms like Gram "knew things," or that she was someone who had the "gift." That way, everyone was left to fill in the blanks on their own.

Every part-time storyteller and gossip always loved talking about Gram Watson's magic book. Some said it was bound in human skin, but that variation of the story was only brought out at Halloween. Most claimed the book gave Gram all the knowledge and power she needed to succeed at anything she wanted. As magic books go, most reckoned it was about as powerful as they come.

Several people around claimed to have seen the book with their own eyes, but no one listened to such gossip. "I reckon a book like that would blind any of the rest of us," Miss Ida Lee theorized one morning before church when the subject came up again.

"I heard there's all kinds of love spells in that book," Bud Jenkins replied with a grin.

"I wouldn't know anything about that," Miss Ida Lee blushed as she turned back around in her pew.

Perhaps the most famous incident in Nelson's Holler happened when Doc Peters started up his practice in town and spent the next three months without any patients. His predecessor had warned him about the "witches" who lived in the hills and the fact that the locals by far preferred spells over shots. One day, fed up with having his patients siphoned off by some crackpot, Doc Peters stormed out of his office to confront who he'd deduced to be the leader of this coven, Gram

Watson. He took his pickup all the way out to her house, the entire time rehearsing the words he was going to use on this old busybody who thought she knew better than he did. He thought he might even throw in a curse word or two for dramatic effect, but then remembered his position in the community and reconsidered.

Doc parked his truck on the dirt road near a little trail that led to Gram Watson's cabin. He stepped out, adjusted the suit that he'd gotten as a graduation present from his parents, then took to the trail. As soon as he hit the dirt, he felt a pull at his pants and heard a ripping sound. Doc Peters swore under his breath as he gently worked the fabric from the clutches of a big blackberry cane he knew hadn't been there seconds ago. With a hole in his trousers, Doc continued down the trail, angrier than ever. Before reaching Gram Watson's cabin, the poor doctor was stung by a wasp on the bridge of his nose, stepped in a pile of cow manure, and walked right through five large spider webs. And, to top it all off, it had started raining.

When Doc Peters got to Gram's front porch, he looked like he'd been dragged through hell and back. He halfway considered just leaving the whole thing alone, but he'd come too far to give up now. With a shaky hand, he knocked loudly on the wooden screen door to the cabin. He winced in pain as he pulled away his knuckles, full of little splinters. This time he couldn't contain his rage and swore loudly into the cloudy sky above.

"I don't take kindly to that sort of language," he heard from behind him.

In the doorway was an old woman, ordinary enough with her gray hair pulled back into a bun on top of her head and floral apron covered in flour. "You Gram Watson?" Doc asked, picking splinters out of his knuckles.

"Sure am, and by the looks of it, you must be our new doctor."

Gram led the man inside the cabin and sat him down at her kitchen table with a cup of coffee and a cinnamon roll. Every time his anger boiled up and he started to air his grievances, Gram would do or say something to distract him until he found himself laughing and even smiling while talking to her. "Gram, I have to admit something," Doc said, mouth full of cinnamon roll. "I came up here to tell you off for taking all my patients, but I just can't seem to find the words anymore!"

Gram just laughed with him. "Oh well, my cinnamon rolls always seem to help sweeten the situation."

Doc laughed again and sipped on his coffee. "And I've got the folks back in town telling me you work all kinds of spells and rituals up here. Oh! And that you've got this magic book as big as a dictionary and made from human skin that gives you powers or knowledge or, hell, I don't know ..."

Gram stepped away from the table while the man was rambling on and returned with a black leather book about as big as a Bible. She placed it in front of her on the table. "Well, it ain't as big as a dictionary," she laughed, "And it's certainly not made from human skin."

Doc Peters sat flabbergasted and staring at the magic book. "So it's … It's real?" he whispered, as though he didn't want Jesus to hear him.

"It's right here, Doc," Gram replied, smiling. "I have a lot of old remedies, recipes, and things I've written in it over the years. If only all them gossips down in town knew I bought my diary here at Bill Martin's pharmacy!" She burst into laughter and slapped the top of the table.

Doc Peters had gone from hating this woman, to somehow really liking her, to now thinking about how he could steal that magic book. He reckoned with his college smarts and city upbringing he could easily distract the old lady and just run off back to the truck with it. He began his clever distraction by accidently knocking his cup of coffee off the table and onto the floor beside him. "I'm so sorry!" he shouted as he stood and wiped his pants with a napkin.

Gram just laughed, shook her head, then grabbed a towel from the kitchen. "It's just spilled coffee, darlin'," she said, bending down to clean the mess off the floor.

Doc took the opportunity to grab the book off the table and slip it underneath his suit jacket, between his belt and butt. He apologized some more as the old woman picked up shards of the broken cup. Then he feigned looking at his watch, saying he had to get back to the office. He'd almost made it off the front porch when he heard Gram hollering behind him. "You no good thief!" she shouted as she busted completely through the closed screen door, hammer in hand.

Doc Peters bolted off the porch and into the woods, thinking he'd be able to lose her easily before circling back around to the truck. As fast as he ran, he heard Gram close behind him the whole time, cursing up a storm. Doc only stopped when he hit the creek. Gram stopped a few yards behind him, still waving the hammer around as she caught her breath. "Don't do anything stupid now," she wheezed.

Doc Peters looked at the creek, then back at Gram. It can't be that deep, *he thought to himself as he stepped into the water.*

Gram shouted behind him and charged forward like a longhorn steer. Doc tried running across the creek, but the algae-covered rocks got the best of him and he fell into the cold water. He felt Gram Watson's hand grab and pull him to his feet again. She searched him for the book as he struggled to get his bearings. He finally gave in and reached for where he'd stashed the tome underneath his suit jacket. But it wasn't there. "Must have slipped out when I fell in," he said with a worried look.

"You clumsy idiot!" Gram yelled, slapping the man hard on the shoulder.

Legends abound throughout Nelson's Holler about what happened to Gram Watson's magic book. Several ginseng hunters I met claimed to have found it in an old creek bed, but they also said they burned it up in a fire lest the devil take their souls. Others have spun similar yarns about having found and destroyed the book, and there are even those who have claimed they sold it to some antiquarian collectors from the city. Despite the number of stories, no substantial evidence has ever been produced, and Doc Peters refuses to talk about the whole matter to this day. Most right-thinking folks in the area say the whole incident at the creek was all a distraction, cleverly planned by Gram Watson to get folks from town off her back. What really happened, they say, was that Gram secretly passed the book to some well-meaning stranger who was out in the hills collecting stories and remedies. But who really knows what's the truth …

OZARK MAGIC

Magic in the Ozarks is a complicated subject. Practices of traditional healing are shrouded in thick layers of secrecy and outright lies that you often have to sift through to get to some notion of the truth. This sifting action has historically been aided by the built-up trust between the storyteller and the listener. "We always lie to strangers," as the famous Ozark saying goes. This sort of trickery or misinformation is rarely based in any malice, but rather in the deep need to protect the culture, sometimes—ironically—even to the detriment of the culture itself.

This intense, almost religious need for secrecy can be traced back to the first hillfolk who flocked to the Ozarks from Appalachia in the early years of the nineteenth century, after the forced removal of the Osage to Oklahoma by President Andrew Jackson. These groups consisted mostly of small hillfolk families who would choose to settle in the Ozark Mountains not as communities but as clans, often separated from each other by great distances. This isolation created a need for families to rely upon each other and each other alone. Many of our folkways, most especially traditions around magic and healing, derive from within these isolated family groups and clans. For every remedy or recipe, there's about a hundred other variations across the Ozarks from family to family. I always like to say that there are as many practices as there are practitioners in the Ozarks. Because these traditions were once so rooted inside family lines, they were often only passed down through blood relatives. Historically, this made it near impossible for outsiders to gather any information unless they were willing to put in vast amounts of time and effort to build up trusting relationships with hillfolk families, as was the case with famous Ozark folklorists like Vance Randolph, Mary Celestia Parler, and Otto Ernest Rayburn.

Magic was once held with great suspicion in the Ozarks, especially amongst more conservative families. The word *magic* was almost always synonymous with witchcraft, and therefore also with harming, stealing, killing, and other malicious acts. Healers had to walk a very fine line with their own magical work to ensure that they weren't suspected by the community of being a witch. These individuals often hid their practices behind words and phrases like *praying, trying, curing,* or even just simply *working.* These clever euphemisms still let the public know that they were a healer, but they shifted the individual away from any incriminating acts. At the end of the day, though, healers were still at the mercy of public opinion, and one bad review could land an individual with some deadly serious accusations.

This situation of magic in the Ozarks is much more complicated than the tall tales, fireside stories, and theories from nonpractitioners have led us to believe. The truth is that magic in the Ozarks has always existed, and it is much more in a gray area than we have historically liked to believe. This magical power itself was—and still is—seen by hillfolk as an overwhelmingly neutral force in the world. It's often compared to and viewed as inseparable from nature itself and is intimately tied to features of the natural world, especially those untouched by humans. This neutral magical force is described in the same ways one might describe a fearsome thunderstorm or wildfire. As one healer told me, "We work with nature, not against it … If lightning strikes a tree and it catches on fire, was that evil? How can a flood or storm be evil? It's the same with our work."

This natural magic can be harnessed and manipulated by certain individuals who are either born with the gift, passed it from another, or who find it through encounters with certain magical entities, usually in the wilderness. As told in many fireside stories, this power can come as a gift from the Little People, capricious Ozark fairies who are often considered trickster spirits of nature. Lineages often form as this power is passed from one hand to another.

In the old days, there were many taboos around passing the gift. For example, it could only be passed down "across sexes," meaning male to female or female to male. There was a taboo surrounding age as well, wherein an elder could only pass the power to someone younger than them. Sometimes the power had to stay within families, so it was once very common to find grandmothers passing their gift down to grandsons or granddaughters.

My favorite analogy for this inborn power likens it to a pitcher full of water. A practitioner is born with a certain amount. Sometimes it's very little in the beginning; other times the pitcher is completely full from birth. Sometimes you can fill your pitcher by being passed some "water" or by finding it in nature amongst inhabitants of the otherworld. Sometimes, it's said, your pitcher can even be filled up by divine forces themselves. Regardless of how it's filled, your "water" can be poured out as well. A common belief in ages past was that every time a person heard your secret verbal charms, some of your power was lost. For this reason, healers and witches still often repeat their charms under their breath or behind their hand to retain their power. When the time is right, you can pour a little of this "water" into your apprentice's cup, or you can pour it all at once and enter retirement. The fact remains that the more power you give away, the less you're left with. This natural magical energy has always been seen as something very tangible for Ozark practitioners; something that can be found, something that can even be stolen, and something that can always be lost.

MODERN MAGIC, MODERN MAGICIANS

Most practitioners in the Ozarks today no longer hold to the old division between the healer and the witch. Many healers I've met proudly refer to themselves as witches and to their practice as witchcraft. This modern trend of reclaiming the symbolism and title of the witch has only quickened the evolution of Ozark folk magic into a tradition that now incorporates many diverse practices in its canon. But the tradition has always been like this. There's never been a single giant tome or user's manual called "Ozark Magic." Our customs and traditions have always been a mishmash of lots of different practices and beliefs, all rolled together amongst isolated families and clans. We have to remember this as we talk about any traditions or folkways. These practices aren't static, and they never have been, despite the often idealistic portrait painted by folklorists and anthropologists. The Ozarks aren't stuck in time; we're always changing, always growing.

More and more modern healers and witches in the Ozarks work within the gray or neutral realm of magic. Another phrase for this is someone who "works with both hands," meaning they practice magic that incorporates elements from both the right- and left-hand paths. This refers to the traditional, cross-cultural delineations for work that either fits well into conservative, mainstream society (right-hand magic) or that intentionally goes against the current (left-hand magic). Magical practitioners in the Ozarks have often taken nature as their example and happily include practices for both healing and retribution, as you will find in this spell book. Most modern practitioners still have a code of ethics, however. Think of these as general guidelines based on much larger cultural beliefs and worldviews, not as a firm set of rules as found in traditions like Wicca, for instance, with the Rede and Rule of Three. Like I said before, there are as many practices as there are practitioners in the Ozarks.

This modern code includes, for example, notions of consent in any work for love or relationships. Most of the practitioners I've met have a firm rule against bending anyone's will for any reason. Some have even said that, try as you might, magic can never make anyone do something they don't already want to do. This doesn't mean that practitioners don't still conjure up some creative solutions to problems of will, however, especially when it comes to matters of the heart. A worker might choose to "smooth the road" instead, as one witch told me; this means working to remove obstacles so that whatever natural love or affection is present will grow unhindered. But as a rule, one should never attempt to blindly manipulate another person against their will. In my own personal practice, I approach any requests for love or relationship work in a very similar way. My motto is "If it's meant to be, then let it be." At the same time, if love isn't already present, even as the tiniest seed, it cannot possibly grow. This also extends to breaking apart relationships, which has historically been the realm of the folkloric witch. Sometimes a relationship needs to be broken up! Sometimes people need a little magical push to tear themselves away from toxic or abusive partners, and sometimes that toxic partner needs a little push too.

I've yet to encounter a modern Ozark healer or witch who has admitted to outright hexing anyone they choose. Nor have I met anyone who uses their power to steal from or trick others without good reason. And that's the key phrase to remember: without good reason. Sometimes hexing needs to be done, perhaps in situations where a person is causing harm to others around them. In this case, their power might need to be diminished in order to allow others to heal. Or their power might be diminished so that they themselves can have space to heal.

This is a worldview that's always been known to Ozark magical practitioners, but it's rarely talked about. In the old days, any inkling of left-handed practices (of which there were many in such a conservative culture) could land a person with the label of witch and, ultimately, isolation from the community. Today, people are much more likely to talk about their more "fringe" or left-handed practices, especially those in younger generations and those living in urbanized areas of the Ozarks. For these modern practitioners, a group in which I include myself, divisions between so-called left-handed and right-handed practices are actually seen as a hinderance to a person's natural ability. Without these strict separations, a witch is able to work far more dynamically to face any problem that comes their way. A witch then becomes an embodiment of nature itself, which both gives and takes at will.

AN EVER-GROWING SPELL BOOK

As you no doubt can imagine, putting together a book of Ozark spells and rituals has been an incredibly complicated process. Not just the process of sorting through hundreds of recordings and scribblings from all my travels, but also working from my own memory. This selection of spells is by no means everything there is to discover in the Ozarks, past or present. It's a sampling of common information at best. There are still practitioners who prefer to work in the old way; that is, keeping all their information secret and inside their own minds. Many believe that by writing down a spell or charm, you risk killing the magic. I've even met some old-timers who didn't like the idea of writing down a simple recipe, believing the resulting food might not taste as good afterward. This has been a struggle for me as a practitioner. I don't know how many times I've gone round and round with myself debating whether or not I should publish this information. It never gets any easier, but I've finally found a balance between my life as a writer and my life as a practitioner.

Over the years I've had the great fortune of being able to work with some amazing healers and witches. But I've also been able to branch off and develop my own practice and work. This path has led me into some interesting areas and has given me a cache of rituals, spells, and remedies specific to my own lineage, if you want to call it that. I wasn't given the opportunity to study at my granny's knee like others, nor did I inherit practices passed down through a family for generations. When it comes to Ozark magic, I've had to become my own family, and you can too. Clear a path for yourself through the wilderness of confusion like our ancient ancestors did. Listen to those with knowledge to offer, but more importantly, learn to listen to your own intuition. Maybe you're someone who naturally knows how to lucid dream, or maybe you create spontaneous rituals using plants and ingredients that shout out to you in that moment. Maybe you whisper homemade prayers while stirring up a hearty stew, or maybe you metaphorically plant those who need healing in with the vegetables and herbs in your garden so that as they grow stronger, so too will those in your heart. No matter how your own magic might manifest, know that it is fundamentally your own to embrace, tweak, change, and, of course, pass on to others.

The first and most powerful meditation within the Ozark folk tradition is that magic is everywhere. Everything we see bears the spark of magical inspiration. For some, this force can be drawn back to one ultimate source in a divine being. For others, this force acts as a unifying ground for all things that exist. Think of it like a patchwork quilt, where each strip of fabric might depict a different shape, color, or form, but it is ultimately part of the same work: the quilt itself. Don't worry, I won't get too philosophical here. All this is to say that in the Ozark worldview, all things in life are sacred; all things are imbued with the same magical energy. From a tall waterfall, to a blooming bloodroot flower, to baking biscuits on a Sunday morning, to laughing with friends … All of it is sacred, and all of it is divine.

Don't let this book dominate your work, but instead let it be a starting point from where your own path, intuition, and family or lineage traditions can grow. Where your own words might work better than mine, use them! Or if you'd like to substitute certain plants in a spell for some you have on hand, go right ahead! In the Ozark tradition, your connection to the practice and your intention are the most important parts of any ritual or spell. Everything else is just a useful symbol to give a little more lift to the work. Ozarkers have always been crafty folk. As one healer told me, "Someone with the gift should be able to do just as good work in an empty jail cell as they can in their own kitchen."

In the end, the magic is inside of you. Let the spell book of your own spirit grow endlessly, and may your works benefit all beings.

SPELL ENTRY STRUCTURE

You'll find that all of the spells, rituals, and recipes in this book have a similar entry structure to make it easier for you to incorporate these practices into your own work. The beginning of each chapter includes specific correspondences for the area of magic discussed within the chapter. Protection work, for instance, is traditionally associated with the planets Mars and the Sun, the zodiac signs Aries and Taurus, and the days of the week Tuesday and Sunday. These general correspondences will help you get a sense for how these specific outcomes or magical goals fit in to the much broader realm of celestial correspondences and how they've been used by Ozark practitioners.

Each individual entry also includes guides to help you gather specific ingredients as well as any magical considerations that might be appropriate, e.g., suggested moon phases, zodiac signs, etc. Entries then offer a step-by-step instruction on performing the complete spell or preparing the remedy. Any variations in ingredients, timings, or phrases will then be offered, and each entry ends with any extra notes on the subject. These notes include any interesting facts about the history behind the spells as well as a deeper look at certain symbols that are used.

The following is the structure for all workings in this book.

- **MAGICAL TIMING:** Suggested time to perform the spell or create the remedy. This timing includes moon phases, days of the week, then zodiac signs. Some entries might only offer part of these timings. It should be noted that these timings are just suggestions, not firm rules. Some healers work strictly within these magical timings and others don't abide by them at all. If working with the moon but not the zodiac appeals to you, then go for it. The full timings listed should be seen as the most optimal time to perform the ritual or create an amulet, but these are often difficult to adhere to. By choosing even one of the suggestions, you will add a great deal of natural magic to your work.
- **INGREDIENTS:** Suggested ingredients to include in the spell. These ingredients can be replaced with others that hold the same correspondences. Suggested variations on ingredients are also listed as a part of the spell entry, where they might exist.
- **CAUTIONS:** Words of warning for any potential hazards of the spell or spell ingredients. This will only appear in applicable spells.
- **SPELL:** Instructions on how to perform the specific spell / ritual or how to make an amulet or tool. Instructions should be read through completely at least once before beginning the spell. This will prevent missing steps or performing certain actions out of order.
- **VARIATIONS:** Any variations on ingredients, words, or steps that can be inserted into the spell as alternatives to what was listed originally.
- **BIBLE VERSE:** Because the Bible has been such an important source of magical knowledge for more traditional Ozark workers and healers, I will include any verses that can be used instead of the words listed in the spells. All Bible verses listed in this book will be from the New Revised Standard Version.
- **NOTES:** Interesting facts about the folklore or symbolism contained within certain spells.

Chapter 1

MAGICAL CONSIDERATIONS

A MORE DETAILED LOOK AT Ozark magical theory can be found in my first book, *Ozark Folk Magic: Plants, Prayers & Healing*, but I wanted to include brief descriptions of some of the more important considerations here, as they will pop up in many of the spell book entries. Of course, remember that these are just suggestions, not firm rules to follow.

A great metaphor that I was once given by a very wise Ozark witch is of a river. Now, you can really move any way you want to while in the river, but the easiest way is going with the current, not against it. A ritual or spell is like this. We begin with only our innate power and intention. Going with the flow of nature—meaning working within certain timings, like moon phases, seasons, and zodiac signs—is like floating on your back in the current, headed toward your destination. Adding on top of that certain items, ingredients, verbal charms, prayers, and other considerations is like building yourself a boat instead of just floating on your back. Working with the grain of nature, not against it, has always been a vital part of Ozark folk magic, and that is represented throughout this spell book in the suggested magical timings and ingredients you will find in the spell entries.

SYMPATHETIC CONNECTIONS

The real heart of Ozark witchcraft and healing is in the unseen magical connection made between the practitioner and the target of their work. Practices that utilize connections like this are sometimes lumped under the heading of *sympathetic magic*, or the Law of

Sympathy, a phrase coined by Scottish anthropologist and folklorist Sir James George Frazer in his work *The Golden Bough*. Sympathetic magic practices can be seen worldwide in a number of folk traditions. This Law of Sympathy can be divided into two subcategories: the Law of Contagion and the Law of Similarity. The Law of Similarity might also be called the "like cures like" method, which sees the use of certain plants, minerals, and even animal bones as being connected to the shape or form of the ingredient. For instance, heart-shaped leaves can be used both in love magic as well as in medicines for the heart or blood. Also, teeth from animals that are known for their large tusks, such as the pig or boar, can be worn as amulets for preventing toothaches.

The Law of Contagion posits that an invisible connection can be made with another person by possessing and manipulating certain identifying materials from that person. The most common materials used include hair, fingernail clippings, blood, urine, and even clothing scraps. By magically manipulating these materials, the practitioner is able to manipulate the individual themselves, even when they are not physically present. According to many theories of sympathetic magic, these connections will last indefinitely until the materials rot away, until the materials are taken back by the owner, or until the connection is severed in some way, usually through magical means.

In Ozark folk magic, identifying materials can be divided into various categories based on how powerful the items are at creating a strong and long-lasting bond with the targeted individuals.

- **FIRST LEVEL (BEST):** Items from the physical body of the target, e.g., hair, nail clippings, teeth, spit, urine, blood
- **SECOND LEVEL:** Items that have touched the target, e.g., clothing, bedsheets
- **THIRD LEVEL:** Other items associated with the target, e.g., footprint, shadow, name
- **FOURTH LEVEL:** Pieces from the person's house, e.g., shingles, furniture, pipes, kitchenware, dishes

The third-level items are some of the most interesting because of how they are collected. For example, footprints can be dug up out of the dirt and taken back home to be used as an identifying material in a ritual. Shadows are collected by sticking a nail or honey locust thorn (*Gleditsia triacanthos*) into the ground through a person's shadow while they aren't looking. The nail or thorn is then removed along with the shadow. Names are collected either by using a written signature from the target or by magically capturing their name, a method that has given rise to the so-called Ozark "superstition" of never answering to your name being called unless you can see the person calling you. This is done using an ordinary bottle with a cap or stopper. Open the bottle while you are near your target. (They must not see you or this won't work.) Call out their name and wait for them to answer. Once they answer to their name being called, close the bottle. This can then be used as identifying material in your rituals.

This sort of magic was once thought to be strictly the domain of witches, at least according to folklore. The witch, having stolen away some of their victim's hair, would then stick it inside of a poppet—or a *spite doll*, as they are called in the Ozarks—thereby creating a magical stand-in that could be tortured or even killed. That's not to say this method wasn't ever used by practitioners in the Ozarks for hexing or cursing; it almost certainly was, and still is in some cases. What's much more common, however, are healers who use these connections to perform remote work on their clients. In these cases, a local healer might only need a little bit of a person's clothing or even just a name in order to create a lasting connection. This has long been a part of traditional Ozark practices of magic and healing. One old-timer I met, in his late seventies when we first spoke, told me he suffered from terrible back pains when he was younger and consulted a remote healer a few hours away. He said all the healer required was for him to write her a letter and she could use that to work on him. Only a few days after sending the letter off to the strange woman, his pains began lessening and lessening until they were completely gone.

As telephones became more and more common across the Ozarks, followed by the internet, social media, and teleconferencing programs like Skype and Zoom, magical practitioners began to create these important sympathetic connections with their clients in more creative ways. Creating this magical "cord," as it's sometimes called, is the basis for even the most basic Ozark spells and rites. For instance, in a common ritual to help grow your good luck and personal success, a person goes outside and digs a hole at the base of a living oak tree. After repeating a certain verbal charm, they then spit into the hole three times before filling it back up again with dirt. In this case, the individual is using their own identifying materials in the form of spit to sympathetically connect their good luck, which they hope to grow, with the ever-growing life force of a strong tree.

Just as sympathetic connections can be created, they can also be broken or severed. This is usually done by a healer on behalf of their client who they believe might have been hexed or cursed. Alternately, a healer whose work has successfully been completed might also want to break the sympathetic connection they created with their client and dispose of their identifying materials, lest they fall into the wrong hands. This magical severing is accomplished in a number of ways, and often individual practitioners will have their own unique rituals. For example, one healer I met had a special knife she used for these severing rites. Another would take his client to a river or spring and wash them with the water and certain mountain herbs. In general, cleansing rites often have the overall aim of severing any magical cords that might be connecting the afflicted individual to an enemy, spirit, or other agent of evil.

MOON PHASES

Working with the phases of the moon is often the easiest way to empower your spells and rituals. Ozarkers have long been connected to these cycles, and not just in healing and magic. Farmers and herbalists knew that the power or life force of a plant waxes and wanes with the phases of the moon. As the moon's light grows, the energy of a plant rises into its aerial parts, and as the moon wanes, the energy returns to the roots. That's why all hillfolk know to pick spinach on a full moon and potatoes on the new. Likewise, medicinal plants or *yarbs* are still almost always harvested according to this theory.

Moon phases can also influence healing and magic work. Generally speaking, the waxing moon is used whenever any work aims at growing, building, or making stronger. An example of this might be having a client drink a certain herbal concoction during the waxing moon to build their health, or tying a loved one's name to a red candle and burning it for a certain number of days during the waxing moon in order to mend a broken relationship.

The waning moon is a time of banishing, diminishing, shrinking, or lessening. A common Ozark cure for warts is to rub a cut potato on each of them, then bury it in a graveyard during the waning moon so that as the moon's light disappears, so too will the warts. The waning moon is also a time of cleansing, particularly in the case of severing sympathetic connections or removing hexes.

The full and new moons are usually designated as stopping points for specific rituals. For example, a ritual for removing a hex might have someone bathe in a certain mixture of mountain plants during the waning moon, using the next new moon as a stopping point for the work. These points are also often used for one-time rituals that seek to utilize a connection to the moon at its most powerful. Creating tools or amulets is often done on the full moon, when the innate magical power of nature is seen as being at its most potent. The full moon is also used for divination, especially using trance or dream work.

MOON PHASE	ASSOCIATIONS	EXAMPLE WORK
New Moon	• New directions • Severing and breaking bonds • Strong lessening, decreasing, and removing	• Removing malign magic • Cutting bonds and contracts • Severing ties with an enemy
Waxing	• Building • Increasing • Growing	• Bringing in new business • Looking for love • Drawing luck and money to the home • Bringing in health after illness
Full Moon	• Strong increasing, building, and growing • Protecting	• Protection • Divination for the diagnosis of an illness
Waning	• Lessening • Decreasing • Removing	• Healing illnesses and curses • Decreasing power of another

ZODIAC SIGNS

As with moon phases, connecting to zodiac moon and sun periods has also been used for both magical and mundane purposes in the Ozarks. For example, each part of the body from head to toe is said to be connected to a certain zodiac sign. An image of these correspondences, often called the Man of Signs or the Zodiac Man, has been used since the Middle Ages to demonstrate this theory. Certain healing processes are often scheduled to fall on a day when the moon is in the corresponding or opposite sign. Farmer's almanacs have long included these "best days" in their pages, providing readers with advice on everything from when to have surgery to when to cut their hair.

Often, spells and magical rituals will also incorporate this special timing into their instructions. Each zodiac sign has a corresponding purpose or domain, so by performing certain works on days that correspond to the purpose of the ritual, the power is heightened. For example, Scorpio moon days are often used as times for banishing work, in particular working against an enemy or breaking a curse. Likewise, a sign like Libra might be used for work pertaining to the law, courts, or justice. A detailed list of these correspondences and many others can be found in *Ozark Folk Magic: Plants, Prayers & Healing*. It should be noted that zodiac moon days, a much smaller increment of time than the sun periods most are familiar with, are generally favored by Ozark practitioners when formulating spells and rituals. Zodiac moon days are easy to find through many different online sources and astrological apps, as well as in the tried and true farmer's almanac, of which there are many versions still being published today.

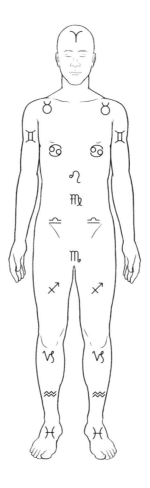

DAYS OF THE WEEK

To round out our discussion of magical timings, we can also use the days of the week to add some extra power to our work. As with the zodiac signs, each day of the week has a corresponding purpose or domain. These correspondences are usually taken from the planetary signs associated with the day. For instance, Friday is connected to the planet Venus and has traditionally been used as a day for work focusing on the home, relationships, cleansing, and love. Likewise, the planet Jupiter rules over Thursday and is connected to the law, wealth, opportunity, and optimism.

On very rare occasions, you'll find a healer or magical practitioner who will calculate days when all three of these timings—moon, zodiac, and day—will be in perfect alignment. For me, however, I often find it's hard enough just getting the right moon phase, let alone all of the other factors. It's important to remember that these are just aids to your magical workings, not firm rules. Let them help where they can, but don't pass up doing important work just because the timing isn't exactly correct.

DAY OF THE WEEK	ZODIAC SIGN	PLANET	ASSOCIATIONS
Sunday	Leo	Sun	• Wealth • Prosperity • Protection
Monday	Cancer	Moon	• Dreaming • Divination • Emotions • Astral travel • Subconscious
Tuesday	Aries/Scorpio	Mars	• Wrath • Vengeance • Physical energy • Strength • Vitality • Competition
Wednesday	Gemini/Virgo	Mercury	• Healing • Communication • Connection to others • Trickery • Deception • Illusion
Thursday	Sagittarius/Pisces	Jupiter	• Politics • Law • Opportunity • Knowledge • Enlargement and expansion
Friday	Taurus/Libra	Venus	• Love • Healing/forming relationships • Harmony • Physical pleasures
Saturday	Capricorn/Aquarius	Saturn	• Relationship to authority • Self-discipline • Boundaries • Limitations • Restrictions • The otherworld • Spirits of the dead

RECHARGING AMULETS AND WARDS

I often see practitioners of Ozark folk magic making the fatal mistake of neglecting the magical objects that they spent so much energy creating. In almost all cases, even those from a more traditional time, physical objects and amulets created for everything from protection to drawing in love or luck require some amount of physical or spiritual upkeep in order to keep running. Even the simplest of Ozark amulets, the buckeye nut, needs some care. These have long been carried as wards against all manner of illness and malign magic. Traditionally, a buckeye charm is recharged by the owner rubbing their thumb in the groove on one side of the nut or by oiling it with "nose grease" collected on the nut by rubbing it several times across one's nose.

As one mountain witch taught me, amulets and wards are like batteries. When you first create them, you fill them with your intention and energy, but over time they run out as they work to fulfill the purpose you entrusted them with. Recharging these items then becomes a must, unless you just want to decorate your home.

The process for this recharging varies depending on who you talk to. For the most part, though, recharging by anointing the object with certain liquids is common in the Ozark tradition. These liquids are different from person to person, but in my own practice I like to use an all-purpose recharging spray made from one cup of gin and twelve drops of camphor essential oil. Gin connects to the cleansing power of the juniper tree (*Juniperus communis*), the Ozark variety being the red cedar (*Juniperus virginiana*), which is actually a juniper, despite the name. Camphor has long been used in the Ozarks as a substance that purifies both worldly and otherworldly contagion. This spray is also great to have on hand for whenever you need to cleanse sickness or negative energies from the home. I recharge my amulets and protective wards every full and new moon, but always recommend to students to at least recharge them every new moon.

While this spray is a great all-purpose recharging liquid, you can really use whatever is on hand. Alcohol is often used, either straight from the bottle or in the form of perfumes. A lot of modern practitioners use popular perfumes like Florida Water or Hoyt's Cologne, which can be purchased at most metaphysical stores. Both of these have entered the modern Ozark practice by way of interactions with Hoodoo and Southern Conjure, as well as Latinx folk traditions like Curanderismo and Espiritismo. Essential oils are also great for recharging items. With these you have the added benefit of choosing specific oils to recharge specific items. For example, camphor oil to recharge protection wards, rose oil for love amulets, and lime for good luck pieces. If you don't have any of these on hand, a few drops of salt water blessed with a prayer or words of intention will work just as well.

PLACES OF POWER

Ozark healers and witches often seek to connect to the stream of innate magic found in certain natural sites, what I like to call *places of power*. These invisible streams are usually located in places of extraordinary beauty or presence in the forest landscape. Places of power might include natural springs, caverns, waterfalls, ancient trees, large boulders, ancient rock piles, etc. These places often attract tourists because of their grandeur or beauty. For this reason, Ozarkers (magical practitioners and common folk alike) are sometimes extremely secretive about the exact location of these sacred spots. I've met many families who have kept sites like these completely secret, the location being passed down only when a person is old enough to hold the knowledge. In one case, it was a swimming hole that was famous for its healing waters. I was finally taken to the site one summer day after many long conversations with the family. The deal was that I could go and see the waters, but I'd be blindfolded there and back so that the exact location could remain secret.

It's often healers and witches who first find these places of power. Because of their gift, Ozark healers are said to be drawn to these streams of magic like metal to a magnet. I have felt this pull before. One time, I was wandering an old logging trail through the woods when I suddenly felt a pull in my chest toward the south, off the trail. I ignored it at first and continued on my way, but I soon developed a sharp pain in my head that would only quit when I turned south. I took this as an omen I shouldn't ignore, so I turned and bushwhacked through the underbrush for about half a mile until I popped out at a large, turquoise-blue creek with a waterfall cascading down off of a bluff above me. I knew then that I was being pulled to a place of power. It came to me just as a feeling. There weren't any grand signs from heaven above or a voice shouting in the wilderness. It was just a feeling deep in my gut that this place was sacred. I sat for a long while and listened to the song of the waterfall, then I finished by taking a cleansing bath in the pool below. For me, sacred places like this can provide a much-needed recharge for our energetic stores, not to mention they are also usually homes for spirits of the land who may even offer up some knowledge to a worthy visitor.

Other practitioners utilize these sacred sites in a number of ways. Traditionally, many healers took their clients to these spots to receive blessings or cleansing work. Others kept these locations completely secret, only known to themselves, but they might bring back items from the place of power to their home in order to incorporate them into their ritual work. For example, spring water, cave rocks, certain healing plants growing around an ancient tree, etc. Nowadays, it seems there are fewer and fewer places of power that haven't been discovered by tourists or used in some way to make money. So many old trees have been cut down, mountains leveled, and springs plugged up. But if you're in the know, you can still find some hidden spots, even on commonly used trails. Some of my favorite magical locations in the Ozarks are connected to tourist areas, but usually away from trails where no tourist would want to hike.

Modern healers and witches utilize these places of power in ways that are very similar to our elders' methods. Some take their own clients to these sites to receive some of the invisible power; others use plants or water from the spot in their work back home. Some even use these places of power for gatherings with other witches and healers, a common feature in the old Ozarks as well, but in a different form. I've heard tales from old folks about the witches Sabbath, or a gathering of witches, usually high up on the top of a mountain or in a dreaded cedar break. Most often these stories have been passed around by nonpractitioners, of course. I once met an older healer who had many Ozark tall tales memorized. I asked him if he'd ever heard about a "witch mountain," as they say, or the witches Sabbath. He just laughed and said, "Well, I reckon it's all in how you look at it. I go to a monthly potluck with some pretty nice witches that don't fit the stereotypes." The old man started to chuckle. "We do meet on a mountain, though."

One person's potluck around a powerfully magical waterfall might be someone else's infernal witches Sabbath, I suppose. Any way you choose to look at it, gathering in these magical groves and sacred sites is still an important part of practitioners' lives in the Ozarks, even though we're far more connected to each other today than our ancestors were. In the old days, meeting up with other healers and practitioners was a rare occasion, but I can imagine it must have been deeply affirming for isolated individuals to be able to share their knowledge in a safe space. For many of us even today, the validation we receive from gathering out in nature with other like-minded individuals is a bolstering force for our work.

WITCH TREES

Throughout the spell book you will no doubt see me mentioning witch trees. This concept is also addressed briefly in my first book. As this is an important part of Ozark ritual work, I'd like to discuss the idea a bit more here.

Witch trees have long had a bad reputation in Ozark folklore. The very name itself recalls the stereotypical image of the hag, using certain cursed trees in the forest for her arcane rites. Today we should read *witch tree* in a very different way. Essentially, these trees could also be called sacred trees, holy trees, etc. and have been in certain folk traditions around the English-speaking world. We Ozarkers still use the phrase *witch trees*, albeit more lovingly these days, to refer to certain species of trees that have long associations with spirits, magic, healing, and the otherworld. Witch trees have developed their reputation for a number of reasons, many of which were borrowed from the Indigenous people of the Southeast when our proto-Ozark ancestors were still in the Appalachian Mountains. Common Ozark witch trees include sassafras, pawpaw, red cedar, sycamore, redbud, dogwood, and of course the witch hazel.

SASSAFRAS (SASSAFRAS ALBIDUM)

To begin, sassafras is a truly magical tree. Its leaves and roots have been used medicinally and magically for centuries. Some of you have had a cup of red sassafras root tea in the springtime. You might not know, however, that sassafras was also one of the original ingredients in root beer. Smell a cup of sassafras tea and you'll immediately make the connection.

Sassafras, as well as its cousin plant the spicebush (*Lindera benzoin*), are both host plants for the beautiful spicebush swallowtail butterfly (*Papilio troilus*) and the promethea silkmoth (*Callosamia promethea*). At certain times of the year, you can see these trees full of swallowtail butterflies, giving them a very eerie appearance, especially when considering that in Ozark folklore, butterflies are often considered spirits of the dead returned to visit the living. For this reason, Ozarkers have long called sassafras a witch tree and many still protect these trees as sacred sources of magic and a link to the otherworld.

Sassafras is a tree that's always associated with water in the minds of Ozarkers. This is partly derived from the fact that the tree prefers moist soil along creeks and rivers, underneath the shadow of the dense canopy above. Because of this watery association, there's a taboo against burning any part of the tree. Sassafras prefers to work with cleansing and purification rites, in particular, washing at the river in the springtime after a big cup of hot sassafras root tea.

PAWPAW (ASIMINA TRILOBA)

Pawpaw trees have also been associated with spirits of the dead in Ozark folk belief. From what I can tell, this mainly stems from the smell of the rotting fruit that often piles up at the base of the tree in the late summer. While pawpaw fruits are delicious and have a more pleasant smell when ripe, they take on a terrible smell when left on the ground. It's attractive to many forest critters but has been likened to rotten flesh or rancid meat by many I've met.

This is then mixed with two other characteristics: one, the sharp, peppery smell of the bark and leaves, often used as a natural insecticide; and two, the zebra swallowtail butterfly (*Protographium marcellus*), which loves to eat and hang out in pawpaw trees, giving it the same otherworldly associations as the spicebush swallowtail does for the sassafras.

Pawpaws are often used as trees for petitioning spells, some of which you will find in this book.

RED CEDAR (JUNIPERUS VIRGINIANA)

Red cedar is, for many Ozarkers, the easiest witch tree to find, and it is the most powerful plant of protection and cleansing in the forest. This tree has deep roots in both Indigenous and European cultures. Where many families from the Old World might have used common juniper as smoke for cleansing and protecting the home, they found an equally powerful cousin in the New World with the red cedar. As I've mentioned before, red cedar is a misnomer. It isn't actually a cedar at all but a juniper, specifically *Juniperus virginiana*, or eastern red cedar in the Ozarks. For students of European folk magic in America, red cedar can be much easier to come by than juniper, making it a good replacement in certain spells and rituals.

In the Ozarks, red cedar trees often grow in what we call *breaks*, or large areas of forest filled with nothing but red cedar trees. Because of the oils in their foliage and roots, much like other evergreens, they naturally kill other plants on the forest floor, apart from mosses and the occasional wildflower or shrub that can handle the conditions. What is left is a large area of open forest apart from these massive red cedar trees. This gives the break an eerie appearance, especially at night or in the morning when the fog rolls through. In the Ozarks, cedar breaks have long had associations with witches, demons, and spirits, all of whom are said to love hanging out in these areas.

There are other folk beliefs about red cedar, like it is always terribly bad luck to transplant a red cedar into your yard. I've talked to several old-timers who still firmly believe this, but they say that if a cedar pops up naturally, that's all right. There's something about the act of transplanting the tree that incurs the bad luck. Some people also say it's bad luck to keep red cedar boughs in your home apart from during the twelve days of Christmas. I talked to a healer once who used red cedar a lot in her practice and had drying branches all over her house. I mentioned this folk belief and she told me that she never had any bad luck, but that she thought the old taboo might have been spread by practitioners trying to keep the tree sacred.

SYCAMORE (PLATANUS OCCIDENTALIS)

Sycamore trees often also go by the name *ghost trees* because there is a belief that spirits of the dead are known to congregate for meetings around sycamore trees. This folk belief then expanded to include witches, often thought to join in on these spirit meetings. Once a tree is big enough, its thin outer bark begins to naturally peel off in places and fall to the ground, revealing a bright white inner bark that stands out beautifully in the forest landscape. As one old Ozarker said to me, this makes the tree "look like old dry bones stickin' up out of the ground." Another reason the tree has associations with the dead.

Bark of the sycamore tree comes off the trunk in large sheets sometimes, and these sheets of bark are said to be used by witches to write out their spell books, although I've never known anyone who had one of these sycamore tomes. What I have found is that many modern practitioners use this bark in place of paper for certain rituals and amulet making, especially those that are meant to rot away quickly as part of the ritual process.

REDBUD (CERCIS CANADENSIS)

The beautiful redbud is a feature across the Ozark landscape. It's one of the first trees to bloom in the spring and makes these ribbons of tiny pink flowers all across its bark and branches, creating a burst of color in the otherwise sleeping forest. European varieties of redbud were given the name *Judas trees*, a title which passed into Ozark folk belief as well. It was said that Judas Iscariot hung himself on a redbud, thereby cursing the tree to always have twisted, gangly branches and bloodred flowers in the springtime. Because of this association, Ozarkers have viewed the redbud as a witch tree, specifically one that should be avoided. That is, unless you're a magical practitioner, in which case there are many rituals and spells that utilize the power of the tree.

The redbud is often used in love magic. This seems to have stemmed from a connection to the tree's heart-shaped leaves and pink flowers. The genus name *Cercis* comes to us from the Greek word *kerkis*, which was the word for a weaver's shuttle, often made from the wood of redbud trees. This is an interesting personal connection I like to make with the redbud tree as a weaver of magic, specifically when it comes to dreams and trances.

DOGWOOD (CORNUS FLORIDA)

Dogwood trees bear a similar biblical curse to the redbud tree. It's said that the cross upon which Jesus was crucified was made from a dogwood tree. Therefore, after the crucifixion the tree was cursed to never be a mighty tree. Unlike the other trees in the forest, dogwoods would only have twisted, short branches and flowers that formed in the shape of a cross.

Despite this curse, the dogwood has a long history of use in medicine and magic. Ozarkers once called the tree *wild quinine* because its bark was used to help quell malarial fevers before true quinine, derived from the South American *Cinchona* tree, could be brought to the area. Carrying a piece of bark from a dogwood was also used as a protective ward against rabid dogs, especially in the "dog days" of summer, ruled by the Sirius star system, when dogs were believed to be extra susceptible to catching rabies. There's also a legend about a group of Ozark witches who could transform themselves into booger dogs using a potion brewed from the dogwood tree. Boogers are legendary Ozark creatures said to appear as solid black animals and are often believed to be so-called witches in disguise. There are many types of boogers, but all are solid black versions of regular animals, including booger dogs, booger cats, booger rabbits, booger possums, and even booger cows. The word *booger* comes from the same origin as *boogie* or *bogie*, as in the boogieman.

Several magical practitioners I've met still use dogwood as a petitioning tree for blessing and healing. One healer in particular tied a strip of white cloth to the dogwood in her yard for every client she worked on.

WITCH HAZEL (HAMAMELIS VIRGINIANA) AND "OZARK WITCH HAZEL" (H. VERNALIS)

Probably one of the most widely known witch trees in the Ozarks is the witch hazel. Ozarkers will often say the "witch" in witch hazel points right to the power of the plant, but it actually comes from the Middle English word *wyche*, from the Old English *wice*, meaning "pliant." I usually keep this information to myself, especially when I'm talking to stubborn old-timers.

Because of its associations with magic and witchcraft, the most famous use for the witch hazel in the Ozarks is as dowsing rods. Dowsers are often called *water witches* or *witch wigglers* in the Ozarks. Despite the name, their practice is almost always seen as more of a science than magic, and few dowsers have ever been accused of witchcraft. Most often, dowsers will use their witch hazel rods to locate underground water sources for wells, but I've also heard about dowsers for all sorts of things from dead bodies to buried treasure.

Witch hazel wands are used in other magical and healing practices as well. For example, one witch I met used a stand of witch hazel shrubs that grew beside a creek near her house as petitioning trees and would tie lengths of white string in their branches for various purposes. Another practitioner I met always stirred his homemade herbal infusions with a witch hazel stick he kept in the kitchen, believing the inherent power of the plant would transfer into the medicine.

—

Many of these folk beliefs involving witch trees can be easily incorporated into any modern magical practice, for example, using leaves, flowers, roots, bark, etc. from a witch tree in a ritual or as an ingredient in an amulet. These are excellent trees to use as alternatives to listed trees and ingredients in many of the spells in this book. So, for example, if a spell lists a pawpaw tree as a part of the ritual, you can easily use a redbud or dogwood instead if that is what you have available to you. Also, the real magic of witch trees is in their power as guiding spirits and helping aids. The simplest ritual could be tying a strip of cloth or some string in the branches of one of these trees along with a prayer or blessing. Another method might be simply offering some water, a handful of food, or some tobacco to the tree in exchange for a prayer or petition answered. A traditional Ozark food offering for spirits of nature or the dead is a mixture of equal parts uncooked oats, barley, and cornmeal. The possibilities for these sacred trees, as with places of power, are limited only by your own intention and imagination.

SMOKE VERSUS SPRAY

Using what is on hand has always been a vital part of Ozark folk magic and healing traditions. Using smoke has ancient origins going back to our prehistoric ancestors, when they first harnessed the power of fire. Much more recently, smoke has traditionally been a part of hillfolk day-to-day life as a result of wood-burning stoves and fireplaces. Speaking in practical terms, Ozarkers likely first began using smoke from certain plants like red cedar to help keep away flies, mosquitos, and other biting insects that would have been common pests in the cabin. By extension, smoke also quickly became an important part of ritual work for magic and healing. One healer described her daily red cedar "smoking" as another form of "sweeping clean" the house. The smoke is a very physical presence, and because of this, clearing out smoke through open windows and doors after the ritual can be seen as a way of also clearing out the illnesses, hexes, and other unwanted energies that are carried with it. Also, because smoke does have this very physical aspect to it, it has traditionally been used as a symbolic way for prayers and other intentions to be carried upward, or into the otherworld, on behalf of the practitioner.

Spells involving smoke or incense can easily be altered, however, in case you are sensitive to either of these components. The easiest alternative is to create a spray instead of a smoke. This is made from a combination of plant ingredients and alcohol. Simply put, you're going to be making a tincture, except instead of using it internally, you're going to use it as a spray.

The formula for this spray is an easy one to remember. Begin with a quart-sized glass canning jar with a lid. Fill the jar up halfway with dried or fresh plant matter, chopped, making sure to use equal parts of all plants included in your mix. Once your herbs are in the jar, fill it up the rest of the way with any alcohol that is at least 40 percent ABV or 80 proof. This includes most vodka, gin, rum, and even tequila or brandy. The choice is up to you, although I usually go with vodka or gin. Vodka is a "clean" alcohol that doesn't add much of its own smell or leave behind a stickiness like you can get with rum, tequila, or brandy. Gin is good to use because it's traditionally made using juniper berries (*Juniperus communis*), which have long been associated with cleansing and protection magic.

Let your plant-alcohol mixture steep for at least a week, but you can go longer if you'd like a stronger concentrate; at most, let the mixture steep for a month. Shake your jar as often as you can to make sure all the plant matter is exposed to the alcohol. After at least a week, strain the liquid into another glass jar. Mix this tincture concentrate half-and-half with water in a spray bottle. You can also add any essential oils that would be appropriate for the specific spell you are working.

You can also make a nonalcoholic version of the spray by using hot water instead of alcohol. Bring water to a boil, then let it cool slightly. Pour over your herbs in a mason jar and let this steep for up to thirty minutes. Strain the liquid, then use it straight or dilute it half-and-half with water. Use within a week.

You can get some more life out of your water infusions by keeping them in the refrigerator, but they will start going rancid after a couple weeks. Also note, an alcohol spray will dry quickly on your wards and amulets as opposed to water. If your charms are staying wet, reduce the amount of spray you use. I've had charms go very moldy from using water sprays, so be careful!

BURNING RITUAL MATERIALS

Several of the following spells involve burning certain ingredients and materials as a part of the ritual. This can sometimes be an area of concern for practitioners in determining safe locations and tools for dealing with ritual fires. Sometimes items are burned in a simple candle flame, in which case all that is needed is a firesafe dish to catch any of the smoldering ash. In other spells, you'll find me recommending charcoal briquettes for burning materials. I find this method to be the easiest and quickest way of making a ritual fire, especially if you don't have a large amount of space for a firepit. Small, portable grills are widely available and relatively inexpensive. These allow for a safe place to burn your materials without taking up too much space on a small patio or even a balcony.

The simplest technique for burning materials with charcoal is using a portable grill. Depending upon the type of charcoal briquettes you're using, you may or may not have to add lighter fluid to get them going. Some charcoal already has this added and you should be able to light the briquettes using just some paper and matches. Other types include incense charcoal, which is generally "self-lighting," meaning all you have to do is hold the charcoal in a flame using metal tongs and it will light.

Traditionally, most Ozark homes had woodstoves or fireplaces which made burning ritual items an easy task. That's not the case these days. Many modern practitioners I've met have set up firepits and other burning spots in their yards, but for those with limited space, the grill method has been very popular. Another setup I've seen is made up of a large cast-iron skillet, usually one that's rusted or no longer suitable for food. The cast-iron skillet is placed on top of two or three bricks for support, depending on how big the skillet is. This makes for a great container for a small fire or layer of hot charcoal. Just make sure you're using cast-iron! Stainless steel often warps under high heat, and non-stick pans will leave you with an awful, smoky mess.

In some cases, burning materials might not be an option at all. Ozark folk magic has many other methods of disposal to offer. In rituals where an enemy or illness is targeted and then burned away, you can also bury your materials or throw them in a moving body of water like a creek or river. Let your methods adjust to your life, not the other way around. One healer I met told me about when she was at university and couldn't even light candles in her dorm room. She created other methods for herself that were just as powerful as some of the more "traditional" ones. She learned to write curses on toilet paper that she flushed down the drain, and she blessed her space with essential oils dropped on cotton balls as a diffuser instead of using incense. Today there is even a wide variety of battery-powered candles in all sorts of shapes, sizes, and colors which can easily be used if needed. Ozark people have long been known for our ingenuity and creativity, especially when it comes to our magic.

CANDLES

Candles have always been a part of Ozark ritual work. Originally it would have been simple beeswax or paraffin taper candles that were kept around the cabin for very practical use, then repurposed for magical means. Alongside oil lamps, candles are traditionally seen as being symbolic of light and thereby healing. There's a Bible verse I've often heard used by Ozark healers, John 1:5, "The light shines in the darkness, and the darkness did not overcome it."

With the influx of other systems of traditional witchcraft into the Ozark region, candles have taken on many different shapes, sizes, colors, and purposes. The basic theory remains the same for most traditional Ozark practitioners: lighting a candle or lamp energizes the work at hand. The simplest candle spell I've found involves just lighting a candle and placing it on top of a written petition, prayer, or list of names.

The candles you will find used in some of the rituals in this book are really just suggestions for tools. Where you can use the specifically requested size, shape, and color, please do so, but even if you only have an ordinary scented jar candle, this can be enough. The size and shape of the candle—unless otherwise indicated in the ingredients list—is up to what you have on hand or can easily acquire. Specific colors of candles will be given in the spell ingredients, but if you don't have access to a candle of that color, you can replace it with any you do have; just don't leave out the candle entirely. Colors help focus the power and intention of the work. Like I mentioned in the introduction, magic can be seen as a river. The practitioner is floating calmly down that river. Yes, you can use your inborn power and intention alone, but tools sometimes help us build ourselves a boat to get where we're going a little quicker.

Colors have specific correspondences in Ozark folk magic. These are mostly derived from other much older magical traditions, but some of them have changed and evolved over the years. Many of these you will no doubt recognize if you are a part of any system of traditional witchcraft or magic. These color correspondences are not set in stone, though. If you sense one purpose aligns with a different color than I've listed, you can always swap it out.

COLOR	RITUAL USE
Black	• Retribution • Hex reversal • Ancestors • Spirits of the dead
White	• Purification • Cleansing • Healing • Protection • All-purpose color
Red	• Retribution • Hex reversal • Protection • Love
Pink	• Love • Relationships • Work for fertility and pregnancy
Blue	• Protection
Green	• Good luck • Money magic • Prosperity • Jobs • Law and courts

Common candle types that you can use include tapers, jars, and votives. There are other specialty-type candles that you can purchase at botanicas and metaphysical shops. You can incorporate one of these types into my rituals as well. For example, a love ritual using a red heart-shaped candle, a protection work using a candle shaped like a sword, etc. Jar candles are often easier for beginners because they are self-contained and easy to reuse. If you choose taper candles, or if the ritual requests this specific type, always make sure to have a holder of some kind to ensure the candles don't tip over during the ritual. Votive and tealight candles are also great to use, but again, make sure you have proper holders for whichever you choose.

If you aren't able to use candles with flames, try using battery operated candles instead. These come in a variety of shapes, sizes, and even colors. The symbolism of the candle remains the same although the actual object itself might change.

There have been many debates about whether candles should be blown out or extinguished by other methods. Some say that blowing out a candle, especially those used in magical or ritual work, will shorten the blower's life or somehow negatively affect the work. As far as Ozark practice goes, this seems to be a relatively modern development. Most of the older healers and practitioners I've met never held to such a belief. If you do, however, you can always extinguish your candles using a snuffer or by rapidly fanning your hand near (but not in) the flame until it is extinguished.

MAGICAL WATERS

Ordinary water from your kitchen tap is perfectly good to use in any of my rituals. Ozark healers and magical practitioners have been working wonders with tap water for centuries. With that being said, if you'd like to incorporate some more magically charged waters in your practice, there are a few that are traditionally used in the Ozarks. In many cases with plants, waters, and other ingredients used in Ozark rituals, the more auspicious the object, the more powerful the work. Auspiciousness in the context of Ozark folk belief just means that there was something unusual or out of the ordinary about the ingredient or object when it was collected. For example, one of the most common waters used in Ozark rituals is water that has never seen sunlight. This is usually collected from springs located deep inside dark caverns. This water is seen as being auspicious, or special, because of its unusual quality and location. Caution should be taken when collecting water out in the wild as many natural water sources have been polluted by runoff from industrial parks, farmland, livestock ranches, etc. While this water might be safe for external use, only use water fit for human consumption in magical work that will be drank.

Water collected from ordinary locations can be made into something auspicious or magical through specific timing or connection to seasonal events. For example, water collected at night underneath the full or new moon can be used in rituals connecting to the specific correspondences of the moon at those times. Along similar lines, water collected when the moon is in certain zodiac signs can be used at later times for the specific purposes associated with those signs. Libra water, for example, can be used for rituals associated with the law and courts. Water collected at dawn on the spring equinox is said to be particularly good with love magic. And water collected at midnight on Good Friday is sometimes used in retribution work because it's traditionally believed that at this time, Jesus briefly left the world after his crucifixion; with this in mind, many practitioners believe a person can't be punished for the curses they sling during this time.

WATER	COLLECTED	RITUAL USE
Never Seen Sunlight	• From a natural spring inside of a cave	• All-purpose use
Full Moon	• Nighttime, from a natural spring or well • Nighttime. Water is left outside in a silver bowl or bowl with a silver object in the water	• Work for increasing or growing • Protection • Divination or dream work for diagnosis of illnesses / curses
New Moon	• Nighttime, from a natural spring or well • Nighttime. Water is left outside in a silver bowl or bowl with a silver object in the water	• Work for lessening or decreasing • Breaking bonds / curses • New directions
Spring Equinox	• Dawn, from a natural spring or well	• Love and relationships • Fertility and pregnancy • Beauty (inner and outer) • New beginnings and cleansing
Summer Solstice	• Dawn, from a natural spring or well	• Protection from sunstrokes and heat
Good Friday	• Midnight, from a natural spring or well	• Retribution • Curses • Work with "darker" entities
Christmas Eve	• Dawn, from a natural spring or well	• Protection for the home • Prosperity • Sprinkled on fields in spring for fertility
Thunder/Storm	• Rainwater is collected in a bowl or bucket during the storm	• Protection • Retribution
Mad Water	• From a natural spring or well during the "dog days" of summer	• Curing rabies • Protection from "mad" or rabid dogs

WORKING WITH A PARTNER

Another way to add some extra power to your spells and rituals is by working with another practitioner or even a group. Most of the spells in this book could easily be reworked for two or more people. Try dividing up the verbal charms between your group or assign everyone their own specific piece of the ritual to perform. In this way, you're adding power to power. So long as everyone's intentions are aligned, amazing things are sure to occur.

Working with some extra help doesn't just mean having a living partner at your side; it can include entities of the unseen world as well. Ozark healers and practitioners have long relied on aid from otherworldly spirits and ancestors to help fuel their work, especially in times of spiritual or magical drought where we might need an outside power to come in and help us. Over the years, I myself have developed very intense and personal relationships with my own guiding spirits and ancestors. They aid me in all my work, just like the natural magic of the moon or zodiac signs also aids me. For many Ozark practitioners, receiving a calling or visitation from a guide, or even multiple spirits, marked their initiation on the path.

These guides come in many forms, though, and you need not fit them into any sort of box, especially those that might be uncomfortable for you. Some have found angels, especially the figure of the Guardian Angel, to be firm and fast help with all of their work. Others have found spirits of the land, like the Little People, to work with. The Little People are our Ozark fairies and are an amalgam of traditional fairy beliefs from across Europe as well as from the Indigenous people of southeastern America, specifically the Cherokee, Muscogee Creek, Yuchi, and Coushatta (Koasati). Working with these capricious tricksters is often a dangerous road, as these entities are very unpredictable. There are many stories about healers receiving great power from the Little People, but at the cost of their vision or hearing, for example, or even their own children.

There are also those who use the power of deities from a variety of pantheons or saints, whose power is often easily given to those with faith and whose abilities are well established as a part of religious tradition. Encountering guides from amongst your own ancestors might prove to be a very powerful and meaningful path to tread. Amongst Ozark practitioners, *ancestor* often refers to both blood family and "ancestors of the work," or those healers and witches of the past who have entered into the spirit world and now aid fledglings on their path.

There is such a variety of beliefs about the otherworld and spirits that you no doubt have your own; your beliefs may or may not figure into your personal practice. Allow me to give you my own view, for what it's worth. I believe that humans are embodied spirits. Our spirit is the core of our being, though we so rarely recognize its potential while we are incarnated. When our time on this planet is up, our spirit leaves our mortal body and enters into the otherworld, a mirror of our own reality, where it now not only knows its potential and purpose, but can remember all of its past incarnations as well. As spirits, we are always learning and growing, throughout all of our lifetimes. With each new body we get better and better, wiser and wiser. At some point, we too can become guides for others, just like the ones we connect to in our work. Our ancestors are part of this evolution and progression as well. They come into our lives as guides and sometimes even leave it to be reborn and continue their own work. While they are present, ancestors can be a deeply meaningful way to connect to your work because the ancestors *know* us. They feel the same blood pumping through our veins. They see the mark of family on our spirits, almost like a fingerprint. We are the embodiment of our ancestors, so as we work, they work. As we heal ourselves, they are healed as well, all the way back through our family trees and all the family trees of every rebirth we've ever had.

It's important to know that you don't have to connect to any ancestors that make you uncomfortable. Sometimes our ancestors were murderers, liars, cheats, abusers, and generally not-so-wonderful people in life. It's okay to work stipulations into your ancestor practice on who exactly is invited in and who needs to stay away. Connecting with a guide—whether it's a deity, angel, spirit, or saint—is a great way to help this along, as they can act as a sort of behind-the-scenes protector when you aren't actively working. If Grandma So-and-So who you really hated in life comes a-knocking at your window, don't be pressured into letting her in! At its core, working with the ancestors is about wanting the best for your ancestors, and that sometimes means they need to go away and continue their own healing process without you. In the healing and cleansing rituals I do for myself, I always dedicate the work not only to my own advancement, but to the elevation of my wandering, lost ancestors as well. You can even work this into your own practice. A simple phrase I repeat at the end of my cleanses is, "As I've been washed clean, so let my hurting ancestors be washed clean. As I've been healed, so let my crying ancestors be healed. As my path is clearly lit and free of obstacles, so let my ancestors be guided in their own elevation."

Encountering ancestors and other guides for the first time is often tricky, and there are no rituals to force them to appear. Not in any *meaningful* form, anyway. Necromancers throughout history have been successful in forcing many different spirits to appear, but do you *really* want to start off your working relationship with issues of consent? The easiest way to open the door is to clearly state your intention. This can be worked into a ritual, or it could be just announcing to the otherworld that you are ready for a guide to appear. Make your intention clear and make sure to add your boundaries and stipulations. For example, say something like, "My spirit is ready. The door is open. Let only those guides who wish to aid me in my elevation come forward. Let only those ancestors who wish to aid me in my healing of others and my own healing come forward." The process is simple: open the door, state your boundaries, then wait. Examine your dreams for messages from the otherworld, as this is often a preferred method of communication in early days of the relationship. You can also petition your "big guides"—the guardian angels, deities, and saints who you might work with already as a part of your religious practice—to bring you other ancestors or guiding spirits who might want to help. In this way, these powerful forces for growth and good can act as a gatekeeper to make sure only those spirits who are beneficial to your own advancement are let through.

WORKING WITH THE BIBLE

Religious practices and traditions in general, not just those connected to guides, are another area to consider when working within Ozark folk magic and healing. Historically, much of our folk beliefs and practices have derived from a deep connection to the Christian faith, specifically Protestantism. For Ozarkers, this worldview emphasized a personal connection to the Divine with no need for any mortal intermediary. It stressed memorizing passages and verses from the Bible, either read or heard during church services. Above all else, perhaps, it showed that living simply and in balance with the natural world could be an important part of spiritual development.

All of these factors influenced the folk magic and healing traditions of the Ozarks greatly. Many healers still to this day use no other methods, items, or ingredients in their practice apart from reading verses out of the Bible. As one Christian healer told me, "The Bible gives a person everything they might need to heal and to curse. It's all right there in the words."

With this in mind, folk magicians throughout the centuries have credited certain verses with certain powers. For example, the famous "blood verse" in the Bible, Ezekiel

16:6, "I passed by you, and saw you flailing about in your blood. As you lay in your blood, I said to you, 'Live!'" This verse was used by many to stop blood flowing from an open wound. Likewise, verses from the Bible could be used in powerful acts of retribution and hexing. Psalm 35:23, for example: "Wake up! Bestir yourself for my defense, for my cause, my God and my Lord!"

There are still many practitioners across the region today who incorporate Bible verses and other traditional Christian prayers into their work—often with much success, I might add. For this reason, many of the spells in this book will also include verses from the Bible as alternatives to the spells and verbal charms listed, in the event that you might want to work in this way.

Religion in the Ozarks is a fascinating subject and one that could occupy an entire work on its own. For now I'll say this: folklorists of the early twentieth century, like Vance Randolph and Mary Parler, often noted that while lots of city folk and others around the country liked to label backwoods Ozarkers as staunch religious zealots, most hillfolk didn't identify with anything more than the virtues of hospitality, care for others, protection of the poor, and the simple relationship between the individual and the Divine, whether that was found in a book, building, or out amongst the trees. Religious conservatism has held the region in its grip for many years now, despite the more liberal philosophies of our Ozark ancestors. Indeed, there's something profound we can learn about ourselves by looking to those beliefs of the past, not in any religious way, but in a way that goes beyond those dogmas we establish as mortals trying to scratch out a living in a universe we don't fully understand. The simple notions of kindness, compassion, and care for all things in nature are the Ozark ideals I most love and cherish, and ones that go far beyond any religious leanings.

REPURPOSING HOUSEHOLD OBJECTS

These days, Ozarkers might be more diverse than ever before, but many people have held on to a deep sense of simplicity in their healing work and magical practice. Traditionally, practitioners only used what they could find around the house, grow, or gather on the land in their work. This was less of a philosophical notion and more a practical measure, as most hillfolk didn't have the money to spend on items for specific purposes and exotic ingredients, and even if they did have the money, there were no stores around to buy from. Many modern witchcraft traditions have made good use out of the wide availability of specialized tools and ingredients, not only at local metaphysical stores and botanicas, but also from online sources. There's nothing wrong with utilizing these sources, as long as it's done with respect for the cultures from which these items and ingredients were derived.

As for me, however, I like to stick with the old Ozark tradition of gathering from the land and repurposing items from the home in my work. For me, this practice goes beyond just the practical and connects deeply with the belief that really all a person needs is their power and intention. I've found this philosophy amongst healers and witches across the Ozarks, from both older and younger generations. Tools and ingredients are then just ways of adding extra magical energy to the work, or ways to better focus your intention, sort of like using a magnifying glass to examine the intricate shapes, colors, and textures in a pinch of sand.

Tools in the Ozarks derive their power from symbolic connections between the object itself and the intended purpose. For example, a broom can sweep your house clean, therefore with the right magical knowledge and intention, it can also sweep a person clean from sickness or hexes. Ozarkers are often very creative when it comes to choosing tools for certain rituals. Don't get frustrated if you don't have a certain tool that is called for in one of the spells. Remember, Ozark folk magic is based in simplicity and connecting to your own inner power above all else. The only separation between an ordinary tool and magical one is the intention of the holder. With that in mind, ask yourself what sort of objects around your own home you might be able to use in place of some of the ones I've listed.

Here are some more repurposed household objects that will pop up in the spell entries throughout this book:

- **AXES:** Used in chopping or cutting rituals to remove illnesses and hexes, specifically from the surface of the skin. Used to magically chop up storms and tornados as they approach.

- **BROOMS:** Used in sweeping rituals to remove illnesses and hexes from the skin of the body. Also used in cleansing rituals in the home whereby evil spirits or bad luck are swept out using a blessed broom. Regular household brooms are most often used, but sometimes also feather dusters, especially those made from chicken feathers, with black feathers being the most powerful.

- **KEYS:** Used in rituals to magically unlock a certain goal or purpose. For instance, unlocking your prosperity or health. Often buried along with open locks at ritual sites as a way of holding the work in a sort of stasis until the object is dug up or rusts away.

- **KNIVES:** Used much in the same way as axes, for magically cutting illnesses and hexes off the skin or clothes of a person. Blades have also been used in rituals for cutting up or preventing nightmares. Granny women have used knives as a way to magically cut birth pains.

- **NEEDLES:** Used both to sew or pin magical ingredients and amulets to clothing as well as ingredients inside the amulets themselves. Along with nails and thorns, needles are added to protection charm bags as a way of halting evil from approaching, either toward an individual or into a home. As one healer told me, sharp objects like these put up a magical fence that evil can't cross unless "it wants to bloody its feet something terrible!"

- **OIL LAMPS:** Used as a way of magically charging petitions or prayers. Practitioners who still use oil lamps as a part of their work will often write their prayers, or prayers for clients, on small slips of paper, then add them to the lamp's reservoir of oil. The theory is that as the lamp is lit, the flame will illuminate the prayers and blessings. I've also seen colored paper used, the color corresponding to the type of work done, with green for good luck, white/red for healing, red for love, blue/red for protection, and black for retribution or cursing work.

- **SCISSORS:** Most often used in rituals for cutting the sympathetic connection between a person and the entity that was determined to have hexed them. I've seen more scissors used for this purpose than I have knives, axes, or other bladed tools. Most commonly, these are ordinary household scissors, but I have encountered a few modern practitioners who use special silver scissors in these rituals, although I have never been able to determine if these tools were actually made of silver.

- **SPOONS:** Used mostly in medicine-making rituals in order to stir prayers and blessings into whatever is being prepared. Some healers I've met have their own special spoons, reserved only for medicine making. One herbalist used a whittled branch of witch hazel, another used a hand-carved red cedar spoon, and one woman I met used a long spoon of undetermined wood that had three cross-shaped holes carved through the bowl.

HARVESTING NATIVE PLANTS

Working with the plant kingdom has always been such an important part of Ozark traditional healing and magic. Plants growing in gardens as well as in the wild would have been treasured as vital tools for the work. As I've said before, hillfolk healing in the old Ozarks relied almost entirely upon what could be grown, gathered, or repurposed around the home.

Today the story is a little different, of course. Many practitioners still maintain gardens with both native and non-native varieties of medicinal herbs, but this isn't always the case for everyone. Practitioners with little access to garden plots or wilderness areas might instead use store-bought herbs, plants purchased online, or plants and herbs from local metaphysical stores. This doesn't mean your work is any less potent than if you were to go out and gather the plants yourself. Work within the boundaries of your own life. That said, if you are interested in growing or gathering your own plants, here are some useful suggestions that I've discovered in my own work.

GROW WHAT YOU CAN

This is always the first level I suggest to my students, especially if they have a garden already or are interested in starting a garden as a part of their practice. Native medicinal plants can almost always be easily started from seed or sprout, and many species are readily available at local nurseries or online. This is assuming you are living in the correct hardiness zone to grow the native plants. If you're wondering about compatibility, you can find a hardiness zone chart in any farmer's almanac.

Ozark native plants are well-suited for the garden and are often perennials that you will enjoy for many years. Native trees and shrubs can easily be incorporated into your landscaping, and most nurseries specializing in native plant species will offer assistance on placement as well as instructions on how to care for your plants. I've had several students who, because of accessibility issues, were unable to hike through the woods to gather native medicinal plants, but who were overjoyed to be able to grow their own. Many varieties don't require a great deal of space and can even be incorporated into container gardens on porches and balconies.

By growing your own plants, you have the added advantage of contact with the plants in all stages of their development. This means that you can formulate specific timings, or "planting by the signs," as the old Ozarkers say. Working in this way connects the plant to certain zodiac signs and moon phases as a way of heightening both the growth and potency of the plant throughout its life. There are still many old-timers around here who swear that plants that are grown alongside the flow of the celestial bodies are healthier and happier, and that the resulting medicines are more powerful. Most farmer's almanacs also provide information about how to plant by the signs.

Gardening your own medicinal and magical plants also allows you to monitor pesticide and fertilizer usage, which might not be the case with store-bought herbs. Regardless of if you grow your own plants or buy them already dried and prepared, you should always take some time to investigate how the plants were grown. Most reputable herb companies will explain their pesticide usage on their websites as well as if the plants are grown within the US or imported from countries who might not have the same standards for pesticides and fertilizers.

GATHER SAFELY AND RESPONSIBLY

If you're like me and weren't born with a green thumb for gardening, wild-harvesting native plants might be your preferred route. Almost all of the plant species I list in my spells can easily be gardened at home, but likewise, they can also be easily found out in the wild. With a few key points in mind, your wild-harvesting trips are sure to be fruitful and enjoyable.

The first thing I always tell my students is to be mindful of where you're gathering your plants from. While you can control pesticides, fertilizers, and chemical contaminants on your own property, you don't have that luxury elsewhere. Gathering from deep woods areas in state parks, national parks, or other heavily forested areas is usually your safest bet. Always make sure there aren't any stipulations about what can be harvest at the location you choose. For instance, many state or national parks have conservation areas where all flora and wildlife are protected. Getting caught with some harvested plants in these spots can land you in hot water. Some locations even fine individuals for removing plants from conservation areas. Most park rangers will be able to tell you the rules of the area and places that should be avoided while harvesting.

Local parks often offer a great abundance of native plant varieties that can be responsibly harvested. Your local Parks and Recreation department can tell you about what pesticides (if any) are used in local parks to ensure that what you're harvesting is safe for consumption. They can also let you know if there are any conservation or protected areas associated with local parks that should be avoided.

It may be tempting to harvest plants from along the side of the road, as these areas are often overgrown and easy to access. These plant varieties often contain heavy metals, however, due to water sources contaminated by vehicle exhaust, trash, and other pollutants. I always advise my students to avoid gathering from areas with heavy vehicle traffic, if at all possible.

Responsible harvesting is one of my biggest pet peeves, and many of my students have heard my endless rants on the subject. The Ozark Mountains are known across the country for our high level of biodiversity when it comes to flora and fauna. There are many plant and animal species that are only native to this one small area of the world. For instance, the Ozark witch hazel (*Hamamelis vernalis*) was once thought to be extinct due to overharvesting of the leaves, which were made into commercial astringents and face washes. Luckily, the species is now out of the endangered zone because of protected conservation areas. This is why it's so important that you are mindful of where to harvest and where you should let the plant species grow unhindered and become reestablished.

A good harvesting rule that I was taught by a very wise granny woman is to count five individual plants before harvesting one. Meaning, if you come across a patch of mountain mint (*Pycnanthemum* spp.) or stone mint (*Cunila origanoides*), you should count five individual plants before harvesting from one. If you need more than one harvest can provide, count out five additional plants before harvesting from another. This ensures that for every plant you harvest, there are at least five others left behind to grow, flower, and spread seeds. This is particularly important when you are harvesting plants like Solomon's seal (*Polygonatum* spp.). It is rare to find this plant out in the wild, and also, you're harvesting the root, thereby killing the entire plant. When harvesting leaves from shrubs like spicebush (*Lindera benzoin*) or the sassafras tree (*Sassafras albidum*), I was taught to only harvest up to ten leaves per tree before moving on. As I said earlier, overharvesting leaves from sensitive shrubs and trees was how our witch hazels almost became extinct.

It should be noted that there's often the temptation to gather more than what is needed because wild-harvesting trips are sometimes few and far between for people. I always advise my students to only harvest what they can use for the next six months—nothing more. Dried plants, even when stored in the cool and dark, only last up to a year effectively before they need to be replaced. If you'd like to extend the uses of your gathered plants, try making alcohol tinctures instead of drying. Tinctures usually have a shelf life of a couple years if stored in a cool, dark cabinet. Just be mindful that tinctures are concentrated extracts, and a dosage will be a lot smaller than with an infusion or tea of dried plant matter.

Remember that you are likely not the only person harvesting plants from a specific area, unless you're off in the deep woods. Because of this, native plant beds can often be easily overharvested if individuals aren't mindful of their practices. Gather what you need on hand, add a little extra, then leave the rest to grow and flourish. In this way, you're ensuring that these plants will be there next year and for many more years to come.

GIVE SOMETHING BACK

For many Ozark herbalists, healers, and magical practitioners alike, it's always necessary to give back offerings of thanks for the gifts that are given by nature and the spirit world. For those who frequently wild-harvest plants, these offerings traditionally include loose tobacco or cornmeal (both traditions inherited from Indigenous peoples of Appalachia), but offerings can also include a whole host of food items, specifically dry grains like oats, barley, millet, spelt, or even dried beans. I like to carry my own mixture of cornmeal, oats, and dried beans to offer in places I've harvested from.

Your offering mixture can be made of anything you choose and doesn't necessarily even have to be food. I've met herbalists who have used water as an offering, and I've met others who offer songs and prayers. You can even do what a good friend of mine does and make an offering of cleaning up trash in areas they harvest from. I will say, in the modern world, this gesture goes a long way in appeasing land spirits.

The important thing to keep in mind is that there should be a real sense of thanks that is offered alongside whatever actions you might perform. An offering given just out of duty or even a sense of fear isn't an offering at all. Always be mindful of your intentions and emotions while harvesting from any location. Traditionally, plants are seen as having spirits of their own, or at the very least, as being living entities that should be cared for and respected. As one of my teachers told me, "If you harvest with love, you'll get a lot of love back."

FORTUNE AND GOOD LUCK

PLANET: Jupiter

ZODIAC: Virgo, Capricorn

DAY: Thursday

COLOR: Green

ITEMS:

- Horseshoe
- Lightning wood
- Rabbit's foot
- Silver dime

PLANTS:

- Beans
- Corn
- Buckeye nut (*Aesculus glabra*)
- Five-finger grass (*Potentilla* spp.)
- Nutmeg
- White oak (*Quercus alba*)

Maintaining good fortune and luck has long been on the Ozarker's mind, since the early days of settlement, when a little bit of divine favor could ensure you and your family's survival in the dangerous wilderness. Hillfolk have had countless measures for growing their luck, as with many other areas of life. These rites, spells, and amulets vary across the region, but there are some common elements that bind together the tradition. The most well-known good luck charm is that of the horseshoe, often hung up above doors (inside or outside) and inside stables or barns as a symbol of prosperity and protection. There's long been a debate amongst hillfolk, however, about whether the two prongs of the horseshoe should point up or down. Some say the prongs should always be up so that the horseshoe forms a symbolic bowl that can hold good luck. Others say the prongs should point down so that the charm's good luck can pour over whoever walks underneath it. So then, which is the correct method? In a sense, they both are! Acts of magic are deeply connected to the practitioner's own spirit and mind. According to the Ozark tradition, the ritual and symbolic ingredients involved don't always matter so much; the work will always follow the trail marked out by your intention.

PERSONAL CHARMS

Ozark hillfolk often still carry a variety of items on themselves as personal talismans or good luck charms. One of these is the silver dime, or the *mercury head dime*, as it's also sometimes called. These coins can be found throughout many different American folk traditions, and the magical power of silver has even more ancient origins. These dimes aren't so common today, and they have mostly been replaced by ordinary dimes in Ozark folk practices. With that being said, I've met several old-timers who swear the new dimes don't work because they no longer contain any silver.

Whether they're of the old variety or new, dimes are connected to the power of the full moon and are seen as charms not only to ensure one's prosperity and fortune, but also as protective wards against all danger. Silver dimes are sometimes carried alongside other pocket change, although the carrier makes deadly sure never to spend such a prized talisman. Some people carry silver dimes in little bags with other good luck charms like a rabbit's foot or buckeye nut, which are both very popular items in the Ozarks still to this day. You can also add a silver dime to any house charm bag to add some extra power to the object. A few believers still wash their silver dimes under the light of the full moon to recharge their power. Others will scoff at this notion, believing the power of the silver dime needs no recharging at all. Which do you believe?

Another talisman is the nut of the buckeye tree, still carried by Ozarkers today, but not just for good luck. Many Ozarkers carry buckeye nuts to help ward off rheumatism or arthritis. Others have claimed they can even help a person keep sexually transmitted diseases away, although the anecdotal evidence around this is very dubious. Famous folklorist Vance Randolph collected this old saying: "No man was ever found dead with a buckeye in his pocket."[1] However, he and I both are very skeptical about that notion. It does attest to the power of this talisman in hillfolks' eyes, however. It's a tradition that is still strong today, and I've met many people in my classes who carry them, even if just for a connection to their cultural heritage. It's often been claimed that buckeyes have to be recharged using the oils from your skin, either by rubbing the nut between your fingers like a worry stone or by rubbing it along the sides of your nose to collect "nose grease." Many of my informants have also said you can never buy yourself a buckeye charm; it must always be a gift from someone else, or it must be found on the ground.

PLANTS OF POWER AND PROSPERITY

Other botanical additions to amulets for good luck include nutmeg (whole and powdered), beans, corn kernels, and the well-known "five finger grass," or cinquefoil, one of several varieties of the *Potentilla* genus. Leaves and bark of the oak tree, specifically the mighty white oak (*Quercus alba*) that is common across the Ozark region, have also long had connections to strength and prosperity, especially when it comes to money and the law. These beliefs likely came with Ozark settlers from their homes in Europe, where the oak has ancient ties to magic. Specifically, the oak tree is often associated with the planet Jupiter, which rules over all things related to law, prosperity, opportunity, and strength. Oak leaves and bark are sometimes added to charm bags to carry while interviewing for a new job or while making business deals. I've even seen oak leaves hung up in the back of shops or stalls at the farmers market to draw in money. Wood from lightning-struck oak trees has traditionally been prized for its magical abilities. Again, this connects back to the power of Jupiter not only in the oak itself, but in the added energy from Jupiter's weapon, the lightning bolt. Lightning wood is often carried on its own as a protective ward, and it is sometimes carved into specialized magical items like spoons, toothpicks, stakes, rings, bracelets, etc.

---

1. Randolph, *Ozark Magic and Folklore*, 153.

RITUAL TO GROW YOUR LUCK AND SUCCESS

MAGICAL TIMING: New moon or waxing moon; Thursday; Taurus or Capricorn

INGREDIENTS:

- Oak tree
- Shovel or spade

SPELL: Go outside and dig a small hole near the roots of an oak tree. Make sure you don't choose a tree that is dying, as you will be connecting directly to the strength and vitality of the tree. Repeat this verbal charm over the hole: "Your roots grow deep! Grow my prosperity! Grow my fortune! As this mighty oak grows strong, so let my luck grow!" Then spit into the hole three times. Refill the hole with dirt and return home.

VARIATIONS: Instead of connecting to a tree, you can also dig a hole either in the ground or in a pot of soil and plant a bulb or other plant. Use the same words and ritual as in the spell section, except instead of the phrase "As this mighty oak grows strong," say, "As this plant grows strong" instead. Spit into the hole, plant the bulb or flower, and let it grow so that as the plant grows and flowers, so too will you grow in health and beauty, and the flowering of your life will be good fortune and prosperity.

BIBLE VERSE: You can replace the verbal charm in the original spell with Psalm 1:3. "They are like trees planted by streams of water, which yield their fruit in its season, and their leaves do not wither. In all that they do, they prosper."

NOTES: If you're using your own potted plant instead of a tree, make sure to take good care of it. It's believed that connecting to a growing plant in this way is a powerful practice and can increase your wealth and health quickly, but it can also cause ruin if you let such a magical plant die.

BUCKEYE CHARM BAG

MAGICAL TIMING: Full moon; Thursday; Capricorn (luck); Aries or Scorpio (protection)

INGREDIENTS:

- Basil essential oil
- Buckeye nut
- Cloth, green

- Hair or nail clippings (your own)
- Needle for sewing, new
- Thread, green, enough to sew the bag

SPELL: For this spell, you're first going to sew a little bag using the green cloth, green thread, and the new needle. Cut the green cloth into two small squares, each about three inches by three inches. Next, take the green thread and new needle and sew clockwise around the edge of the two squares of cloth. You can use any stitch you'd like, but I find a tight whip or edge stitch works best. While you are sewing, repeat this phrase as many times as you can: "Little bag I sew, sew, sew you up! I sew you up strong, strong, strong! Bag never break, break, break! Bag always be filled, filled, filled with lots of money and luck!"

Sew the bag on three sides. Then, with the thread and needle still attached, turn it inside out. Add the buckeye nut and some of your hair or fingernail clippings into the bag, then finish sewing. Once you reach the end, set the stitch with three knots and then cut the string. Anoint with three drops of basil essential oil, then carry it out of sight in your pocket or purse. Anoint with three drops of basil essential oil every new and full moon to recharge.

VARIATIONS: Instead of making a bag from scratch, you can start with a small green cloth bag. Sometimes you can find them with a drawstring top. After filling it with the required items, pull the drawstring closed and seal with three knots. Make sure you repeat the verbal charm in the spell section for each knot. If your cloth bag doesn't have the drawstring top, you can sew it closed with green thread while repeating the verbal charm.

BIBLE VERSE: You can replace the verbal charm in the original spell with Genesis 49:22, 26. "Joseph is a fruitful bough, a fruitful bough by a spring; his branches run over the wall … The blessings of your father are stronger than the blessings of the eternal mountains, the bounties of the everlasting hills; may they be on the head of Joseph, on the brow of him who was set apart from his brothers."

NOTES: Objects that are considered "new" are used a lot in Ozark folk magic to add extra power to the ritual or spell. New items should be "clean," meaning they haven't been used for any other purpose before, but they don't necessarily have to come from a completely new package. For example, a new needle could be one taken from a package of multiple needles. Some practitioners will even destroy an object like a new needle after it's been used as a part of the ritual. One healer I met always took a pair of wire cutters and cut up the needles or nails she used after a ceremony before throwing them in the garbage can. She said it was to ensure someone wouldn't be able to find the needle and "unsew" all her magic.

LIGHTNING WOOD FOR GOOD LUCK

MAGICAL TIMING: Full moon; Thursday; Gemini (gambling) or Capricorn

INGREDIENTS:

- Cloth bag with drawstring top, white or green
- Lightning-struck wood
- Paper square, green, 3 inches by 3 inches
- Pencil or pen
- String, 2 pieces, white or green, 3 feet each
- Camphor, basil, or lime essential oil

SPELL: First, take the green square of paper and write your own full name three times in the center, one after the other, like this:

FIRST MIDDLE LAST

FIRST MIDDLE LAST

FIRST MIDDLE LAST

Then, in each of the four corners of the paper, draw a four-leaf clover shape or a horseshoe so that the prongs of each U shape are pointing out toward one corner, like this:

Choose a piece of lightning wood that's small enough to fit inside the square of paper. White oak (*Quercus alba*) is the best, but oak in general will work. Other lightning-struck trees will do in a pinch. Roll the paper square around the wood, forming a tube with all your writing on the inside, along with the lightning wood. Fold down the top and bottom of the tube to form a parcel. Tie up the parcel securely with the string and then seal with three knots. Then, while holding the parcel in your right hand, say, "As lightning strikes sure and quick, so let money and good luck fill my pockets just as fast!"

Put the parcel into your cloth bag, pull the drawstring closed, and seal the loose strings with three knots. Recharge your bag each full and new moon using camphor, basil, or lime essential oil.

VARIATIONS: If you aren't able to get lightning-struck wood, don't worry. There is an alternative to this ingredient that, while not as powerful, is still pretty powerful. Instead of the lightning-struck wood, you can use a piece of regular white oak (*Quercus alba*) that has been soaked in lightning water. This is made from water placed in a silver bowl (or a regular bowl with a silver item added) that is left outside in the open during a lightning storm. This magically charged water is then collected immediately after the storm and bottled for safekeeping. Soak your oak wood in this water overnight on the full moon, then use it in your bag.

BIBLE VERSE: You can replace the verbal charm in the original spell with Isaiah 60:17. "Instead of bronze I will bring gold, instead of iron I will bring silver; instead of wood, bronze, instead of stones, iron. I will appoint Peace as your overseer and Righteousness as your taskmaster."

NOTES: Some Ozarkers in the past have made amulets directly from the lightning wood itself by choosing a suitable piece and then drilling a hole in one end and wearing it on a string, or even by carving the wood into a shape meant to resemble the magical goal that is sought after. For example, I've seen lightning wood carved into coin shapes for money, swords for protection, hearts for love, etc. It was also once believed that using a toothpick carved from lightning wood would prevent toothaches and that chips or sawdust from lightning wood, when scattered around the walls of the home, would drive away pests like insects and mice.

RITUAL TO OPEN THE DOOR TO PROSPERITY

MAGICAL TIMING: New moon; midnight; Taurus or Capricorn

INGREDIENTS:

- Lighter or matches
- Mistletoe leaves, dried or fresh (*Phoradendron leucarpum*)
- 1 padlock and key, new
- 2 taper, votive, or jar candles, white

FOR THE CLEANSE:

- Pitcher of clean water
- Set of new, unworn clothes
- Towel

CAUTIONS: While European mistletoe (*Viscum album*) was traditionally used internally by herbalists, *this species is very rare in the US*. American mistletoe (*Phoradendron leucarpum*) can be toxic if ingested, especially the berries. Do not consume any part of the plant. Smoke from burning American mistletoe can also irritate the lungs and esophagus. Be sure to wear gloves when gathering and working with the fresh foliage. Dried mistletoe is relatively inert, but the fresh sap can cause contact dermatitis where it comes into contact with the skin.

SPELL: Before beginning the ritual, make an infusion of mistletoe and boiling water. Make sure to do this outside, and cover your face, as mistletoe steam and smoke can irritate the eyes and sinuses. A simple infusion is made from boiling water poured over plant matter. In this case, you can carry your water in a separate container and then combine with the mistletoe once you're outside. When the water has cooled, drop in the key to your padlock and let it set for at least an hour. You can also leave it until you begin the ritual.

Before beginning the ritual, make sure to prepare your cleansing bath that will end the work. Fill a pitcher full of clean water (spring water is the best, but any will do.) You will also need a set of new clothes that you have never worn before. These can be as simple as a pair of shorts and a T-shirt.

At midnight on the new moon, take the key and padlock to one of the doors in your house that leads outside. Open the door and place your two white candles on either side of the frame. These can be taper or jar candles, whichever you'd like; if you're using taper candles, they should be at least six inches long, and make sure to put them in holders so they don't fall over. Your candles can be placed inside or outside the house.

Before lighting the candles, make sure you are inside your house looking out the open door. Lock the padlock and remove the key. Now, light the two candles and say, "I open the lock to my fortune! I open the lock to my destiny! I open the door to opportunities that will benefit many and harm none! I open the door to good luck and prosperity!" After saying these words, unlock the padlock and leave it open on the floor in the doorway.

Some people might choose to do this ritual in the nude from the very beginning; others might wear their regular clothes or a bathrobe that they will then take off once outside. Either way, grab your pitcher of water, new clothes, and a towel, then step through the door to the outside. Once outside, immediately strip off your old clothes and pour the water over your head in three pours. By the end of the third pour, all of the water should be used. After this, dry off with the towel and put on your new clothes. Once dressed again, blow out the candles.

There's long been a debate in the folk magic community about blowing out versus snuffing out candles. In some traditions, candles are always snuffed out, the idea being that by blowing out the candle you are somehow reducing or reversing the power you put into the work, i.e., symbolically "blowing" away the intention. In the Ozarks, there isn't such a taboo, and candles are blown or snuffed out depending upon the practitioner's preferences.

Only when the candles have been blown out can you reenter the house. You can cleanse the key and padlock with red cedar smoke to use again. Take your "old" clothes (or the ones you stripped off) and wash them.

VARIATIONS:

- One common variation on this spell has the worker bury the open padlock and key underneath the doorway that was crossed over. This usually happens before the cleanse with water and the wearing of the new clothes. The key should remain in the padlock when buried, and the padlock should be open. It's believed that as long as the lock remains open, so too will the doorway to your luck and prosperity.

- In a variation on the new clothes part of the ritual, some practitioners will burn the old set of clothes or throw them away. Others claim you have to turn the old clothes completely inside out and then boil them in salt water outside of your house to completely cleanse them. To avoid having to do all of this, some practitioners choose an easier route and just perform this ritual completely naked up until the wearing of the new clothes. It's also perfectly okay to keep the old clothes—just make sure to wash them after the ritual.

BIBLE VERSE: You can replace the verbal charm in the original spell with Psalm 24:7–10. "Lift up your heads, O gates! and be lifted up, O ancient doors! that the King of glory may come in. Who is the King of glory? The Lord, strong and mighty, the Lord, mighty in battle. Lift up your heads, O gates! and be lifted up, O ancient doors! that the King of glory may come in. Who is this King of glory? The Lord of hosts, he is the King of glory."

NOTES: There are several spells in this book that will require certain cleansing acts, and some spells even have cleansing as their main focus. These rituals are very interesting to look at and often involve complicated procedures. The most basic form of cleansing, however, can be performed by pouring clean water three times over the head so that it runs down the body. That's it! In this spell, water is used alongside another common cleansing ritual: changing out clothing. The symbolism behind this act is connected to renewal and rebirth. Just like a snake shedding its skin, we shed our own "skin," so to speak, when we change out our clothes in a ritualistic manner. This act might seem simple, but it has long been used as a cure for some pretty serious illnesses and hexes in the Ozarks.

NUTMEG NUT FOR GOOD LUCK

MAGICAL TIMING: New moon to full moon; Wednesday (begin); Gemini (gambling) or Capricorn

INGREDIENTS:

- Cloth bag with drawstring top, white or green
- Gin or camphor essential oil
- Nutmeg nut, whole
- Silver item

SPELL: This ritual will begin on the new moon and end on the full, so be prepared for some daily attention!

Start by gathering your whole nutmeg nut, silver item, and some gin or camphor essential oil. The silver item can be anything made from silver. For example, I have a little silver bowl a friend gave to me years ago for rituals such as this one. You can also use a silver coin, ring, spoon, chain, or anything else really; you just want to make sure the nutmeg can touch the silver throughout the entire ritual.

On the day of the new moon, place your nutmeg in such a way that it is touching the silver item you have chosen, but you can still get to it. If you don't have a silver bowl, you can place both the nutmeg and the silver item in a regular bowl so that they are contained. Anoint the nutmeg with three drops of gin or camphor essential oil. Gin is a great ritual alcohol to use because it contains juniper, which has long been associated with a wide variety of magical practices.

After anointing the nutmeg, recite this charm: "On a mountain far away grows a rock. On that rock grows a mighty tree. On that tree grows a little nut. Inside that nut grows a little bag. Inside that bag grows a river of gold coins. This nut in my pocket hears my tale and knows exactly what I mean."

After reciting the charm, you will leave the nut touching the silver item. Every day until the full moon, anoint the nut again with three drops of alcohol or essential oil and then recite the charm. On the full moon, repeat this process again, except you will end by putting the nutmeg nut into your cloth drawstring bag and tying the strings closed with three knots.

To recharge, anoint the nutmeg through the bag with three drops of alcohol or camphor essential oil every full and new moon.

VARIATIONS: This same ritual process can also be done for other "lucky" items like a buckeye nut or lucky coin. You can even use a silver dime, in which case you wouldn't need any other silver item as a part of the ritual. If you'd like to use a silver dime, it should be made of real silver, not like modern coinage. These are sometimes also called *mercury head dimes*, as they have the image of the Roman deity Mercury on one side. While these dimes aren't in circulation anymore, you can still find them online or at shops that specialize in coin collecting.

BIBLE VERSE: You can replace the verbal charm in the original spell with Job 42:10. "And the Lord restored the fortunes of Job when he had prayed for his friends; and the Lord gave Job twice as much as he had before."

NOTES: Nutmeg nuts were once a rare item in the Ozarks, likely only ever purchased at the local pharmacy or grocery store and at great cost to hillfolk. For this reason, they are considered lucky or specifically magical items. Like the buckeye, the nutmeg also could act as a sort of worry stone that gradually smooths out over the years. One of my informants showed me the nutmeg he'd carried in his pocket for almost thirty years. I marveled at the smooth surface, almost reflective after being rubbed between the man's thumb and forefinger for so many years. According to folk belief, the power of the nutmeg can rub off on your hands through this action, thereby giving you good luck, specifically at card games and dice.

RITUAL FOR JUSTICE FOR THE WRONGED

MAGICAL TIMING: Full moon; Tuesday; Libra

INGREDIENTS:

- Candle, taper, votive, or jar, green
- Incense charcoal and burner, with metal tongs
- Knife
- Lighter or matches
- String, white or green, 3 feet
- 2 oak stakes, 1 foot long each

JUSTICE POWDER (EQUAL PARTS):

- Cornmeal
- Red cedar berries, dried (*Juniperus virginiana*) or juniper berries (*Juniperus communis*)
- White oak bark, dried (*Quercus alba*)

JUSTICE INCENSE (EQUAL PARTS):

- Fennel seed, dried (*Foeniculum vulgare*)
- Red cedar berries, dried (*Juniperus virginiana*) or juniper berries (*Juniperus communis*)
- Sweetgum resin, or dried bark (*Liquidambar styraciflua*)
- White oak bark, dried (*Quercus alba*)
- White willow bark, dried (*Salix alba*)
- Yarrow flowers, dried (*Achillea millefolium*)

SPELL: This ritual is intended for those seeking justice, either for themselves or on behalf of another. It is particularly potent in cases where justice has been corrupted or when someone has been falsely accused of a crime.

Begin by mixing up your justice powder and incense (separately) so you can have them both on hand. The ratios for the plants are all equal parts, so you can make a small amount of each just for this ritual or you can make them in bulk.

After you've prepared your powder and incense, cut two one-foot-long sticks from an oak tree. Traditionally, white, post, or red oaks are favored in the Ozarks. Black oaks are usually associated with malign magic and should be avoided. The white oak is generally considered to be the most powerful to use.

When you have your sticks, find a flat place on the ground where you will be performing the ritual. Make sure to gather your two sticks, the string, the knife, the incense burner and charcoal, the green candle, as well as your justice incense before you form the ritual circle. For the candle, you can use a taper, votive, or a jar candle, whichever you would prefer. If you're using a taper candle, make sure it is at least six inches long, and also bring a holder so that the candle will sit firmly on the ground during the ritual.

Once you've gathered your items, take your justice powder and face east. Leaning over, pour some powder on the ground, then—moving clockwise—make a complete circle around yourself using the powder. Make sure the circle is large enough to contain yourself and the other ritual items.

After the circle is formed, sit in the center and face east. East is considered sacred in the Ozarks, so all right-handed magic is usually performed while facing that direction. Take your two oak sticks and drive them side-by-side into the ground in front of you, about a foot and a half apart from each other. Tie the string tight between the two sticks, which will collectively form a sort of H shape.

Next, light your green candle and place it a few inches from the right stick, making sure it is far enough away so that it doesn't burn the string or stick. Take your incense burner and charcoal and place it directly underneath the middle of the string. Light your charcoal by holding it over the candle flame using metal tongs. Once the charcoal is hot, add some of your justice incense.

After this, take your knife in your right hand and say these words three times: "Blind Justice, help me today! Let the scales be restored, and let balance be regained! Blind Justice, bring your flaming sword and cut these chains! Blind Justice, bring your flaming sword and let justice be served against my enemies!" (Alternatively, you can also replace "against my enemies" with "for [NAME]," this being the full name of the person on whose behalf you might be performing this ritual.)

After repeating the phrase three times, heat the tip of the knife in the candle flame. Once hot, cut through the middle of the string tied between the two sticks. Make sure to snuff out the strings if they catch on fire, then blow out the candle.

You can dispose of the sticks and string in one of two ways. You can either bury them together in the roots of a white oak tree, or you can burn them to ash and then mix the ash with beeswax. Once hardened, you can place a chunk inside a cloth bag to carry as an amulet.

VARIATIONS: In one variation I was taught, instead of cutting the string with the hot knife you can pull up the two sticks, holding one in each hand with the string pulled tight, and then burn the string using the candle. Similarly, you can break the string by raising up the incense burner while it is smoking and allowing the string to touch the hot charcoal and be singed apart.

BIBLE VERSE: You can replace the verbal charm in the original spell with Proverbs 11:1–6. "A false balance is an abomination to the Lord, but an accurate weight is his delight. When pride comes, then comes disgrace; but wisdom is with the humble. The integrity of the upright guides them, but the crookedness of the treacherous destroys them. Riches do not profit in the day of wrath, but righteousness delivers from death. The righteousness of the blameless keeps their ways straight, but the wicked fall by their own wickedness. The righteousness of the upright saves them, but the treacherous are taken captive by their schemes."

NOTES: This ritual is one I learned from a modern Ozark witch who still had deep connections to her Ozark roots and had learned much at her grandma's knee. Hillfolk of the past had many different methods for enacting justice, especially in cases of blood feuds between families. In one unique ritual I was taught, the family of someone who was murdered could take three nails from the victim's coffin and hammer them into a chunk of wood stolen from a church house. This was then hidden away from sight somewhere in the family's home. It was believed that the spirit of the victim could now act through this charm in order to guide the family to the perpetrator or even enact justice themselves. As long as the nails remained in the wood, the ghost could continue to seek their revenge.

RITUAL TO DRAW CUSTOMERS TO YOUR BUSINESS

MAGICAL TIMING: Full moon; Friday; Capricorn

INGREDIENTS:

- Bowl
- Potted plant
- Silver item
- Water

SPELL: Start this ritual on the full moon, preferably in Capricorn if you can. First, you'll want to have a potted plant of some kind. Make sure the plant stays in your business or, if you work from home, keep it in the area where you do most of your work and planning. On the full moon, put some clean water into a bowl along with your silver item. As in the nutmeg charm, this can be anything made of silver, including a silver dime, ring, or chain. If you can, the easiest way to perform this ritual is to use a silver bowl to hold the water.

Once your bowl is filled, say these words three times, blowing across the surface of the water after each recitation: "A silver moon hangs above; silver moon for luck and love. Bring to me some folks with gold; bring them here until I'm old. When I'm gray and bones are tired, release this charm that was hired."

When you're finished, pour the water onto the plant. Repeat this process along with the verbal charm and blowing action every full and new moon to keep your plant recharged. If your plant happens to die, don't worry! You can just bring another one into your business and repeat the ritual process.

VARIATIONS: Instead of a potted plant, you can also do this ritual with a root, bulb, or seed. Make sure you follow the same procedure no matter what plant you choose.

BIBLE VERSE: You can replace the verbal charm in the original spell with Psalm 82. "God has taken his place in the Divine council; in the midst of the gods he holds judgment: 'How long will you judge unjustly and show partiality to the wicked? Give justice to the weak and the orphan; maintain the right of the lowly and the destitute. Rescue the weak and the needy; deliver them from the hand of the wicked.' They have neither knowledge nor understanding, they walk around in darkness; all the foundations of the earth are shaken. I say, 'You are gods, children of the Most High, all of you; nevertheless, you shall die like mortals, and fall like any prince.' Rise up, O God, judge the earth; for all the nations belong to you!"

NOTES: The witch I learned this spell from told me that you can judge the health of your business by how one of these charmed plants grows. If it's healthy, strong, and slow growing, that means your business will last a long time. If it grows faster than it normally would, that means your business will boom but might not last. And if it begins to die, that means it is taking in some bad luck or hexes directed at your business and you should do a cleansing quickly.

LUCKY CHARM FOR GOOD BUSINESS

MAGICAL TIMING: Full moon; Friday; Capricorn

INGREDIENTS:

- Business card
- Cloth bag with drawstring top, green
- Five-finger grass leaves, dried (*Potentilla* spp., "Cinquefoil")
- Frankincense resin or essential oil
- Incense charcoal and burner, with metal tongs
- Lighter or matches
- Paper square, green, 6 inches by 6 inches

SPELL: As with the previous spell, the perfect timing for making this amulet is on the full moon, preferably in Capricorn, but any full moon will work. On the square of green paper, you're going to place your business card and a heap of five-finger grass. Fold the corners of the paper into the center, then fold the left side completely over, and finally fold the top down to make a small square packet.

Place this packet in your green cloth bag, then tie closed with three knots. Light your charcoal by holding it in the flame from a lighter or matches, making sure to also use metal tongs as the coal will get hot quickly. Once the charcoal is hot, add some frankincense resin and then suspend the bag over the smoke. You can also anoint the bag with three drops of frankincense essential oil instead. Repeat these words three times: "Little Bag, Little Bag, bring me my heart's desire! The moon is full and silver above us; let light shine in my business, let gold fill my pockets, and Little Bag get to work!"

Hang this bag inside near the front door to your business, or if you work from home, hang it in your office or workshop. Smoke with frankincense resin or anoint with three drops of frankincense essential oil every full and new moon to recharge.

VARIATIONS: You can also use red cedar (*Juniperus virginiana*) smoke instead of frankincense, or even smoke from burning five-finger grass. Either of these can also be brewed in hot water like an infusion and then sprayed or dropped onto the bag.

BIBLE VERSE: You can replace the verbal charm in the original spell with Psalm 82. "God has taken his place in the Divine council; in the midst of the gods he holds judgment: 'How long will you judge unjustly and show partiality to the wicked? Give justice to the weak and the orphan; maintain the right of the lowly and the destitute. Rescue the weak and the needy; deliver them from the hand of the wicked.' They have neither knowledge nor understanding, they walk around in darkness; all the foundations of the earth are shaken. I say, 'You are gods, children of the Most High, all of you; nevertheless, you shall die like mortals, and fall like any prince.' Rise up, O God, judge the earth; for all the nations belong to you!"

NOTES: Five-finger grass is so named because the shape of the leaves forms a little hand that curls closed when dried. Because of its shape, the leaves have been used in many Southern folk traditions for magically "grabbing" money or good luck. In the Ozarks, it's sometimes just called "lucky grass," and it's traditional to carry a leaf or two in your pocket for good luck.

RITUAL TO PETITION AN OLD OAK FOR PROSPERITY

MAGICAL TIMING: Full moon; Thursday or Friday; Taurus or Capricorn

INGREDIENTS:

- Beeswax, melted
- Cup of water
- Offering mixture for spirits: equal parts oats, whole barley, and cornmeal
- 3 strands of your hair
- 3 strips of cloth, green, about 1 foot each

SPELL: On the full moon, take the three strips of green cloth and, on one end of each strip, place a single hair from your head (or from the head of the one you are working for, if this ritual is to help someone else). Take and bind the hair to the cloth using a small spoonful of the melted beeswax. Let this cool and harden.

Next, take your three strips of cloth along with a cup of water and small bowl of your spirit offering mixture outside to an oak tree. It's best to choose a tree that is already quite large and very healthy. Avoid trees with a lot of dead limbs or holes in its trunk. Once at the tree, you are first going to greet the tree with these words: "Good day to you, old man in the woods with arms strong and body stout!" Then pour the cup of water on its roots and trunk and say, "A cup of water to refresh you." Take the bowl of spirit offering mixture and sprinkle it around the base of the tree in a clockwise direction, saying, "A bowl of food to nourish you."

After you've done this, tie each of the strips of cloth onto a separate branch. Repeat these words each time: "A task for you to complete, if you will it so." Once finished, return back home and let the old oak work its magic.

I should add here that traditionally, Ozark workers would pick a tree that was either hidden away in the woods or close enough to the house to keep an eye on. The idea being that if someone found the strips of cloth you hung in the branches, they could either remove them, thereby nullifying the spell, or worse—use them in malign magic against you.

VARIATIONS: The spirit offering mixture is my own recipe and can be adjusted however you would like. For me, the three food items represent common nourishing grains of both the Old and New Worlds, as well as the symbolism of the number three. You can use any other food offering that might be appropriate for the specific situation and your cultural background.

BIBLE VERSE: You can replace the verbal charm in the original spell with Proverbs 10:22–24 while hanging the three cloth strips. "The blessing of the Lord makes rich, and he adds no sorrow with it. Doing wrong is like sport to a fool, but wise conduct is pleasure to a person of understanding. What the wicked dread will come upon them, but the desire of the righteous will be granted."

NOTES:

- Powerful trees are often petitioned as helpers in Ozark spells and rituals, especially where the practitioner might not think they themselves would be powerful enough to successfully perform the rite. See the section about witch trees in chapter 1 for a bit more information. While this is only hinted at in the spell section (and it wasn't provided to me by my original informant), the oak tree is being petitioned as a living entity or spirit, not as a sort of natural "battery" full of magical energy. Keep in mind that spirits have personalities of their own. They all have wants, desires, dislikes, etc., so if your ritual doesn't go according to plan, perhaps try asking the tree what would be proper to offer in exchange for its help. Or, when in doubt, try another tree.

- Traditionally in the old Ozarks, this ritual would have used the "plugging" method common to hillfolk magical and healing practices. In this method, a hole would be bored into the side of the oak tree and then filled with a tiny bundle made from a few strands of the person's hair and some beeswax, all wrapped in green cloth. After adding this bundle to the hole, it would then be plugged up using a branch from the same tree. I don't recommend this method today, as boring holes like this can weaken a tree, especially a young one.

A POCKET FULL OF GOLD AMULET

MAGICAL TIMING: New moon; Wednesday or Thursday; Virgo or Capricorn

INGREDIENTS:

- Cloth square, green, 5 inches by 5 inches
- 12 corn kernels, dried
- Frankincense resin or essential oil
- Incense charcoal and burner, with metal tongs
- Lighter or matches
- String, green, 3 feet

SPELL: First, cut out a five-by-five square of green cloth. Starting at the top of the square, trace a large circle, clockwise, with the forefinger of your right hand. Still using your finger, make a vertical line through the middle of the square from top to bottom followed by a horizontal line from left to right. Add the kernels of corn to the center of the cloth square and then say, "Love in my heart, gold in my pockets!"

Blow across the kernels three times, then bring the corners of the cloth in around the kernels to make a small bundle. Seal with the green string and tie closed with three knots. Bless the amulet by smoking it using frankincense resin or by anointing it with three drops of frankincense essential oil. To smoke the bag, first light your charcoal by holding it in the flame from a lighter or matches, making sure to use metal tongs as the coal will get hot quickly. Once the charcoal is hot, add your resin and then hold the bag in the smoke.

Carry this amulet in your pocket, bag, or purse, especially while at work or during an interview for a new job. Recharge every new moon using frankincense smoke or essential oil.

VARIATIONS: I've also seen this amulet made using other important Ozark food staples like beans. One ritual in particular supposedly combined twelve different types of dry beans in the amulet, although I wasn't able to confirm that. I've known many Ozarkers who grow nearly that many different heirloom varieties, so it wouldn't surprise me at all. Dried lima beans and peas, both favored for their green color, are other amulet ingredients that I can absolutely confirm.

BIBLE VERSE: You can replace the verbal charm in the original spell with Psalm 18:20. "The Lord rewarded me according to my righteousness; according to the cleanness of my hands he recompensed me."

NOTES: Corn has long had associations with prosperity and wealth in the Ozarks. At one time, it was a staple of hillfolk diet and is still a major part of our regional foodways. Corn, either in its whole kernel form or as cornmeal, has therefore also featured heavily in the magical traditions of the Ozarks, including work for good luck and prosperity and as an offering food for ancestors and spirits. Several backwoods herbalists I've met make a habit out of offering a little cornmeal to wild plants they harvest as a sign of gratitude to the spirits of the plants.

While similar traditions also exist in many European cultures surrounding staple grains like oats, barley, and wheat, this specific usage of corn would have been introduced into Ozark practice through interactions with the Indigenous people of the Southeast, encountered while Ozarkers were still back in their Appalachian Mountain homeland.

Chapter 3

LOVE AND RELATIONSHIPS

PLANET: Venus

ZODIAC: Taurus, Cancer

DAY: Friday

COLOR: Red

ITEMS:

- Dove's tongue
- Turkey beard/wishbone

PLANTS:

- Violet (*Viola* spp.)
- Redbud (*Cercis canadensis*)
- Yarrow (*Achillea millefolium*)
- Rose, cultivated varieties as well as native roses like *Rosa arkansana* and *R. carolina*, both of which often go by the name of "dog rose" in the Ozarks

Magical work for love and relationships was once a very important part of Ozark life, and it pops up frequently in folk records. In the old days, finding a spouse was just as necessary to survival as learning to grow food or hunt. There are countless Ozark divinations and charms for finding one's true love or future spouse. (Some of these divination methods will be mentioned later on in the book.) The general opinion of love magic has changed in the modern world, however. Fewer and fewer Ozark practitioners know the old marriage divinations or love potions. Some even now refuse to work with matters of the heart or relationships. Because of the current view on love magic, you'll find this chapter to be a little thinner than the others. The spells I do provide here have been built from the intention that this kind of magic should work with the will of nature instead of trying to go against it. You won't find any spells here that aim to manipulate or bend the will of another. If love is meant to be, so let it be.

LOVE CHARMS

Common love amulets across the Ozarks include items specifically made from parts of the native turkey. In all my hunting across the hills and hollers, I've yet to find out why the turkey is specifically associated with love magic in the Ozarks. There are a number of birds here in the mountains that are generally looked on as being magical in some way; these are often called "witch birds" alongside their specific names and are sometimes even thought to be witches or healers in disguise. The turkey is one of these witch birds, and turkeys are given a great amount of respect by hillfolk as sources of food and magic.

Two parts of the turkey's body in particular are used in traditional love spells: the beard and the wishbone. The beard is a tuft of feathers found on the neck of male turkeys underneath their bright red wattle. These beards are often collected by turkey hunters as trophies but can also be pinned on or under a person's shirt, usually somewhere out of sight, in order to attract their true love to them quickly. Likewise, a turkey's wishbone was sometimes hung at the top of a house's front door as a traditional charm to attract a person's love to their home. A far less pleasant charm is mentioned by Vance Randolph in his *Ozark Magic and Folklore*. This practice involves hiding a dove's tongue somewhere in your crush's home. This act was believed to make the person fall madly in love with you.[2]

AMOROUS BOTANICALS

Specific plant species associated with Ozark love magic include all types of violets (*Viola* spp.), redbud trees (*Cercis canadensis*), yarrow (*Achillea millefolium*), and of course roses. Violets and redbud trees are favored on account of their heart-shaped leaves, which are often used alongside rose petals as ingredients in charm bags. The bright pink flowers of

---

2.   Randolph, *Ozark Magic and Folklore*, 169.

the redbud, which are often the first tree flowers to bloom in the springtime, are sometimes also gathered and brewed into potions or worn in the hair to attract the eye of a potential love interest.

The fragrant flowers of the yarrow plant are favored in a number of Ozark spells, not just for love magic. They are also used in traditional cleansing rites as well as in a number of herbal preparations for many different illnesses. The smoke from burning the leaves and flowers has also been used by hillfolk as a powerful fumigation against illness and hexes.

LOVE MAGIC AND CONSENT

Love magic is one area in particular that has changed greatly from the old Ozarks to now. Most magical practitioners today will likely have faced a dilemma about whether to cast a love spell or to refrain. Many of the practitioners I've met flat out refuse to work any magic for love or relationships. The main question I see popping up—and it's one I myself have had to ponder—is of consent in the work. We've all no doubt seen a spell or two that aims at making someone fall in love with you, or perhaps even fall out of love. The Ozark tradition is actually full of them, and they're all interesting bits of magical history to look at. Should they be modernized? I don't think so, and here's why.

My own personal view is that as a witch, I'm only working within the boundaries already established by nature itself. This flow of energy and time is deeper and more mysterious than we can ever fully know. Like my Ozarker ancestors, I'm a firm believer in auspiciousness, that there's a time and place for everything to manifest. If the signs are right and the tokens or omens foretell success, then the work will be accomplished. If not? Well, try again later or find a different route. A worker always needs to be mindful when it comes to any spells or rituals that involve manipulating the free will of another person. This can be love work, or it could even be healing a client. Take, for instance, this situation:

A person comes to you wanting to be healed from high anxiety stemming from a stressful job. They're looking for some magical help to be able to let go and relax. In the course of talking to them and planning the ritual, you discover that there are some other aspects of their lifestyle and habits that might also be contributing to their anxiety. They express to you that they can't change these other things right now and only want work aimed at helping them with the stresses caused by their job. It might be tempting to adjust your work to help cover these other areas as well, but without the consent of your client, is it the right thing to do? As with all areas of folk magic and healing, there's of course no right answer to that question. It depends on the practitioner themselves and what work they're willing to do. I should say, this is an exact situation I've come across in my work. Many, many times, in fact. The common trend these days amongst the Ozark witches and healers I've met—and the view I take in my own work—is that consent is crucial.

Another common request I get is healing a relationship or marriage that is falling apart. I even include a spell in this chapter. When I first started working publicly, these requests always stressed me out. Questions would come up like "What if this marriage needs to end?" or "What if they're lying to me and their partner is actually in a bad situation staying with them?" These are, of course, real concerns to consider with any work you do, even work for your own relationships! Over the years I've developed a less stressful process for myself when working with rituals that might involve potentially non-consenting individuals. This process can apply not only to your work with others, but also to rituals for yourself.

The first thing I do is try and gather as much information as possible to be able to get a really good reading of the truth behind the situation. This is always important, and getting to the heart of the matter will create a much more powerful ritual or spell. For instance, maybe you're doing some magical work for yourself to help heal a relationship. While meditating on the situation, trying to dig down deep to the heart of the matter, you discover that the tension between you and this other person might be caused by an old wound within yourself, not them. The ritual then turns from targeting the both of you to perhaps being just healing work for yourself alone. When the wound is healed, the relationship can begin to heal as well.

After considering the heart of the situation, the work can then proceed as planned. Often, though, there's still some targeted individual who isn't able to give their consent. Whereas before I'd stress over this matter to no end, nowadays I take a much simpler approach. If I'm working with a client, I'm very up-front about my upholding of consent and the alternative spells I work with. Instead of targeting the will of another person, like in the old days, I instead will work a ritual with this intention: whatever is *meant* to happen will happen.

Let's look at a simple, classic love spell. Person A wants Person B to fall in love with them. In a lot of magic traditions, especially those coming out of older folk cultures, the most basic formula would be performing some magical act to bend Person B's will so that they act in a way that perhaps goes against their natural inclinations. But maybe Person A just really isn't person B's type. This is what I mean by having a non-consenting target in the spell. Person B isn't being consulted about whether they want this whole love thing to turn out in the same way Person A wants. Just because we might be more mindful of consent in our magical workings today, that doesn't mean we have to completely scrap our spells and rituals about love and relationships. It *does* mean we might need to work with a different intention. Let's go back to our hypothetical love spell. In this situation, I would craft a ritual aimed at letting love blossom *naturally*, as it is meant to be. If there is perhaps already some love there to grow, then great! But if not, I'm willing (or I encourage Person A to be willing) to let Person B go and live the life they choose.

This approach to magical work doesn't just apply to love rituals and spells. In all the work I do, I try to hold the intention that things will happen naturally, as they should. Again, to go back to the roots of Ozark folk magic, working within the stream of nature is vital for not only a successful practice, but also for personal growth and healing. In fact, as many of the old tales often tell, going against the current set by nature is a dangerous way to travel. As one healer told me, people who work against nature often find nature fighting back at every turn.

RITUAL TO BRING TWO LOVERS CLOSER

MAGICAL TIMING: Waxing moon (can end on full moon); Friday; Taurus

INGREDIENTS:

- Cloth, red
- Lighter or matches
- 2 paper squares, white or red, 4 inches by 4 inches
- Pen, red
- Rose essential oil
- String, red, 3 feet
- 2 taper candles, red, with holders, at least 6 inches long each

SPELL: On a small square of paper, write Person #1's full name and birth date in red ink. Encircle with a heart shape, also in red. On a separate square of paper, repeat this for Person #2.

Take your red taper candles with holders and place them side-by-side on a flat surface, about a foot apart from each other. Place the paper square with Person #1's name underneath the candle holder on the left and the other paper square under the right. Take a length of the red string and make a hoop around the two candles. Tie the strings together, but don't knot them fully, as you will be pulling the string tighter throughout the ritual. Pull the string just tight enough so that it is touching the base of the candles on each side, left and right, making sure it won't be near the candle flame.

Light the candles and say, "If love is in our (or your) hearts, then love let your flame burn bright." Let the candles burn for seven minutes before blowing them out. Leave your setup as is; you will be continuing the ritual for two more nights.

The next night, pull the string a little tighter, bringing the two candles and their squares of paper closer to each other but not yet completely together. Light the candles again, then repeat the verbal charm. Burn the candles for seven minutes more before blowing them out.

On the third night, pull the candles completely together with the string. This time, knot the string tightly three times, binding the candles together. Repeat the verbal charm, then burn the candles for seven more minutes before snuffing out. Take the candles out of their holders, then tie the two squares of paper to them with some more red string and three tight knots. Wrap all of these items up in red cloth, then keep this bundle hidden somewhere in your home.

Anoint the candles and papers with three drops of rose essential oil every full and new moon to keep the magic working. As long as you recharge the bundle, the magic will continue.

VARIATION: In a simplified method, find two stalks of mullein (*Verbascum thapsus*) growing close together in the wild. Name one for yourself and the other for your love. You can also stick some hair from each person in the flowers, sealing it there with a little melted beeswax. Tie the two stalks together with red string and say, "What love has brought together, let no one separate."

BIBLE VERSE: If you are performing this ritual for yourself, you can use Song of Solomon 5:10–16. If you are performing it for someone else, use Song of Solomon 5:10–16 if the target uses he/him pronouns, and Song of Solomon 7:1–9 if they use she/her. You can use either verse and change the pronouns to use they/them.

- Song of Solomon 5:10–16: "My beloved is all radiant and ruddy, distinguished among ten thousand. His head is the finest gold; his locks are wavy, black as a raven. His eyes are like doves beside springs of water, bathed in milk, fitly set. His cheeks are like beds of spices, yielding fragrance. His lips are lilies, distilling liquid myrrh. His arms are rounded gold, set with jewels. His body is ivory work, encrusted with sapphires. His legs are alabaster columns, set upon bases of gold. His appearance is like Lebanon, choice as the cedars. His speech is most sweet, and he is altogether desirable. This is my beloved and this is my friend, O daughters of Jerusalem."

- Song of Solomon 7:1–9: "Your rounded thighs are like jewels, the work of a master hand. Your navel is a rounded bowl that never lacks mixed wine. Your belly is a heap of wheat, encircled with lilies. Your two breasts are like two fawns, twins of a gazelle. Your neck is like an ivory tower. Your eyes are pools in Heshbon, by the gate of Bath-rabbim. Your nose is like a tower of Lebanon, overlooking Damascus. Your head crowns you like Carmel, and your flowing locks are like purple; a king is held captive in the tresses. How fair and pleasant you are, O loved one, delectable maiden! You are stately as a palm tree, and your breasts are like its clusters. I say I will climb the palm tree and lay hold of its branches. O may your breasts be like clusters of the vine, and the scent of your breath like apples, and your kisses like the best wine that goes down smoothly, gliding over lips and teeth."

NOTES: I've seen a similar ritual performed using red candles shaped like men and women. These are common in botanica-based traditions like Conjure and Hoodoo and are now easily available online. Traditionally, regular beeswax tapers would be used by Ozarkers for any candle work.

RITUAL TO HELP STRENGTHEN A RELATIONSHIP

MAGICAL TIMING: New moon to full moon; Friday; Taurus

INGREDIENTS:

- Paper square, red, 4 inches by 4 inches
- Pen, red
- Potted plant or bulb

SPELL: This ritual can be for either a romantic or platonic relationship. The aim is to help deepen your connection with another person, be that a partner, friend, or even family member.

Start the ritual on the new moon in any zodiac sign. Taurus is specifically a good time to strengthen existing relationships. First, write the full name and birth date of both yourself and the one with whom you'd like to have a stronger relationship in the center of the square of red paper like this:

FIRST MIDDLE LAST

BIRTH DATE

FIRST MIDDLE LAST

BIRTH DATE

Then, draw a heart around the names and birth dates in red ink. After this, take the paper and plant it into the roots of a potted flower, bulb, herb, etc. Your choice as to the plant, although I prefer those with large, colorful blossoms. While you work, say, "As this root grows, and as this flower blooms, so may our love grow stronger and stronger every day!"

Repeat this phrase every morning and evening until the full moon. I find adding rituals like this into my daily breakfast and going-to-bed routines works well. Be sure to tend to your plant's needs. It's believed that as its life flourishes or withers, so too will the relationship you have charmed. Be sure to consider this risk before beginning the ritual!

Continue tending to your plant even after the full moon to maintain strength and health within the relationship. If things sour again, you can start this ritual over on the next new moon. One practitioner I met chose to plant her flower out in the garden on the full moon, letting nature take its course.

VARIATIONS: You can also plant your square of paper in the roots of a tree that's already growing strong out in nature. Redbud (*Cercis canadensis*), dogwood (*Cornus florida*), and pawpaw (*Asimina triloba*) trees are all associated with love and relationships in Ozark folklore. You can also use a white oak (*Quercus alba*), which is an all-around wonderful tree used for many different purposes. Just make sure the tree you choose isn't dead, dying, sick, or at risk of being cut down!

BIBLE VERSE: You can replace the verbal charm in the original spell with Psalm 45:7–9. "… Therefore God, your God, has anointed you with the oil of gladness beyond your companions; your robes are all fragrant with myrrh and aloes and cassia. From ivory palaces stringed instruments make you glad; daughters of kings are among your ladies of honor; at your right hand stands the queen in gold of Ophir."

NOTES: Connecting magically to growing plants is powerful work and shouldn't be performed lightly. Traditionally, Ozarkers viewed the bond that was created with certain trees or plants during a ritual like this to be semipermanent. For some, this meant that if you were to connect your luck—or in this case, love—to a growing plant and it died or was cut down, your love and luck might be permanently cursed or damaged. For this reason, choosing the best plant for the work is vital. Make sure you choose a plant that is strong, healthy, and will be long-lasting. Try choosing something that will come back every year, like a bulb or native wildflower. If you're connecting to a tree instead, make sure it's not at risk of being cut down or dying! Using a tree that's on your own property or one out in protected forest land is best.

TWELVE-FLOWER CHARM BAG TO ATTRACT FAVOR

MAGICAL TIMING: Full moon; Friday; Taurus (general use / established relationships); Cancer (family / romantic relationships); Libra (justice system / marriages); Gemini (work / school relationships)

INGREDIENTS:

- Beeswax, melted
- Cloth bag with drawstring top, white or red
- 12 flowers:
    1. Blackberry (whole flower)
    2. Black-eyed Susan (whole flower or petal)
    3. Fire pink (whole flower)
    4. Horsemint (whole flower head)
    5. Lady's slipper (whole flower)
    6. Redbud (whole flower)
    7. Rose (petal)
    8. Spring beauty (whole flower)
    9. Tulip poplar (whole flower)
    10. Violet (whole flower)

11. Yarrow (floret clump)

12. Yellow trout lily (whole flower)

- String

- Toothpick

- Wax paper, 6 inches by 6 inches

SPELL: This powerful charm bag involves finding twelve Ozark flowers, several of which only come out once a year. I asked the woman who gave me the recipe why it was so complicated, and she just replied, "Power demands sacrifice." I will say, if you choose to sacrifice some time for this charm, you won't regret it. This magic is aimed primarily at attracting favor and kindness from everyone you meet, but it can be expanded to include drawing new love toward yourself, healing broken relationships, or even as a protective ward. It might take some time and effort to create, but the resulting amulet will be something you can carry for many years.

Start by collecting all your flowers. I've listed scientific names and the best time to look for these throughout the year in the notes section of this spell entry. When collecting your flowers, you will really be using only one flower head or petal from each plant. In cases where the petals are too small, as with yarrow, you can use a clump of flowers instead. Once gathered, air dry all of your flowers thoroughly, making sure to turn them occasionally to prevent molding. When they are all dry, grind them together into a powder.

Begin your charm making on the full moon. Taurus is a good moon sign to use, but any full moon will work. On a square of wax paper, pour a little melted beeswax, or let a beeswax candle drip until there is a small pool. Add all of your flower powder, then mix with a toothpick to make sure it has all been incorporated into the wax. Let the wax cool slightly and then, using the wax paper, mold it into a ball. Twist the top of the wax paper, then tie closed with a string. You can trim off any excess wax paper at the top. Once your bundle is fully cooled and hardened, you can pop it into your cloth bag and then tie it closed with three knots.

As it was told to me, this charm bag needs no recharging to continue working, but if you choose to, you can anoint with three drops of rose essential oil every full moon.

VARIATIONS: The practitioner who gave me this recipe said that in cases where you might want to draw favor or love from a specific person, you can write their full name on a small piece of red paper and then burn it in a red cedar fire. Once burned, grind all of the ash and mix with your flower powder.

BIBLE VERSE: Read Psalm 22:19–26 while grinding the flowers. "But you, O Lord, do not be far away! O my help, come quickly to my aid! Deliver my soul from the sword, my life from the power of the dog! Save me from the mouth of the lion! From the horns of the wild oxen you have rescued me. I will tell of your name to my brothers and sisters; in the midst of the congregation I will praise you: You who fear the Lord, praise him! All you offspring of Jacob, glorify him; stand in awe of him, all you offspring of Israel! For he did not despise or abhor the affliction of the afflicted; he did not hide his face from me, but heard when I cried to him. From you comes my praise in the great congregation; my vows I will pay before those who fear him. The poor shall eat and be satisfied; those who seek him shall praise the Lord. May your hearts live forever!"

NOTES: The following are flowering times in the Ozarks. You'll of course want to check on availability and blooming times for your local area. These ranges are figured for the Ozarks, so northern Arkansas and southern Missouri, but are also similar to the middle Appalachian regions as well.

BLACKBERRY: May–June

BLACK-EYED SUSAN (*RUDBECKIA HIRTA*): June–October

FIRE PINK (*SILENE VIRGINICA*): April–June

HORSEMINT (*MONARDA BRADBURIANA OR M. FISTULOSA*): April–June; May–August

LADY'S SLIPPER (*CYPRIPEDIUM SPP.*): April–June

REDBUD (*CERCIS CANADENSIS*): March–April

ROSE: Spring/Summer

SPRING BEAUTY (*CLAYTONIA VIRGINICA*): February–May

TULIP POPLAR (*LIRIODENDRON TULIPIFERA*): May–June

VIOLET (*VIOLA SPP.*): March–June

YARROW (*ACHILLEA MILLEFOLIUM*): May–October

YELLOW TROUT LILY (*ERYTHRONIUM ROSTRATUM*): March–May

RITUAL TO ASK A PAWPAW TREE TO BRING YOU TRUE LOVE

MAGICAL TIMING: New moon; Friday; winter or early spring; Taurus or Cancer

INGREDIENTS:

- Beeswax, melted
- Offering mixture for spirits: equal parts oats, whole barley, and cornmeal
- Rose petals
- 7 strands of your hair
- 7 strips of red cloth, 1 foot each
- Violet leaves

SPELL: First, prepare your strips of cloth. I recommend strips that are a couple inches wide and about a foot long. These can be cut, but the traditional method is to tear these strips. Using metal items like scissors is often believed to negate certain magical workings. Once you've got your seven strips of cloth, gather up seven strands of your own hair. The easiest way is to pull them from a brush or comb, but you can also take them directly from your head if you choose.

Next, prepare the rose petals and violet leaves by grinding them both into a semi-fine powder, or as fine as you can get. If you're using fresh leaves and petals, you can grind them together into more of a paste. Either will do just fine, but I find dried plants are a little bit easier to work with.

After you have the strips of cloth and plant mixture ready, melt your beeswax. Then, on one end of each cloth strip, you're going to pour a little wax, sprinkle a bit of your plant mixture, and finally add a single hair, making sure it sticks into the wax. You can also easily use a beeswax candle and let the wax drip onto the cloth strips.

Once you have all seven cloth strips made in this way, take them along with your spirit offering mixture out to a pawpaw tree (*Asimina triloba*). Once located, you will first sprinkle the offering mixture in a clockwise circle around the base of the tree, saying, "Pawpaw, pawpaw, growing strong, growing tall, growing wide. Bring me my heart's true love, as sweet as your ripe fruit in the autumn." Then tie each cloth strip to a different branch. As the tree blossoms and its fruit ripens through the year, it's said that your true love will get closer and closer. By the time the pawpaws drop to the ground, you will have found your true love.

As with the spell for an old oak, try and find a tree that won't be cut down or disturbed. The best option is to use a pawpaw tree in your own backyard, if you have one. If not, you can conceal the strips of cloth in the tree by tying them close to the trunk.

VARIATIONS:

- You can also use red yarn instead of red cloth strips. In this case, you would dip one end of the yarn in the melted beeswax and then gently attach the hair before rolling it in the plant mixture.

- Pawpaws and redbud (*Cercis canadensis*) trees are often used interchangeably for rituals focusing on love or relationships, so you are welcome to use a redbud tree if that is what you have available. If not, you can also use an apple or cherry tree, and this includes the wild cherry (*Prunus serotina*) and chokecherry (*Prunus virginiana*).

BIBLE VERSE: You can replace the verbal charm in the original spell with Song of Solomon 8:13–14. "O you who dwell in the gardens, my companions are listening for your voice; let me hear it. Make haste, my beloved, and be like a gazelle or a young stag upon the mountains of spices!"

NOTES:

- Petitioning certain witch trees for various purposes has deep roots in the Ozarks, and many old-timers still practice the tradition of tying strips of cloth in certain trees as a form of blessing or petitioning for aid from the magical otherworld. Again, this ritual would have originally been performed using the "plugging" method, as explained in chapter 2, but the cloth method is just as traditional, just as powerful, and doesn't damage the tree.

- I specifically mention winter or early spring for this ritual because the spell itself grows with the pawpaw tree you are petitioning for help. If you have trouble identifying trees in the wintertime, I recommend finding a pawpaw in the summer when they have leaves (and sometimes fruit) and marking it with a colored flag or strip of cloth so that you can easily find it later on in the year.

RITUAL FOR A YARROW LOVE POTION

MAGICAL TIMING: New moon to full moon; Friday; Taurus

INGREDIENTS:

- Alcohol
- Bottle or mason jar with lid
- Bowl
- Drinkable spring water or tap water
- Pen or pencil
- Silver item
- Square of paper, red, 6 inches by 6 inches
- Yarrow flowers, fresh or dried

SPELL: Begin this ritual on the new moon, preferably in Taurus. Begin by making the base potion, which you will be charging and blessing during the waxing moon. This is a simple infusion of yarrow flowers in water. The old-timers used to use spring water for all of their potions and magical workings, believing that water coming directly from the ground had its own unfiltered magical essence. You can use spring water, but please be careful about where and how you gather it as many natural springs are now contaminated by chemical runoff from farms or livestock. You can also use bottled spring water or even ordinary tap water with just as powerful results. Remember, intention is key.

Because you are going to be drinking this potion in one sitting, I recommend making a small batch. It might seem tempting to make a large amount to save for future use, but the power of the drink will fade over time. It's best to just make more later on.

Bring a cup of water to a boil, then immediately remove from heat and let stand for a minute to cool slightly. With infusions of plant flowers and leaves, you almost never want to actually boil the material but instead let it steep in water that is just below boiling temperature. Add two teaspoons of dried or fresh yarrow flowers and let this steep for five minutes. Sometimes when you buy yarrow it comes as a mixture of flowers and leaves; this will also work for the ritual.

After five minutes, strain the liquid and then add a tablespoon of alcohol. This can be any alcohol of your choosing, but I recommend an elderflower liqueur, which also connects to love magic, or gin, which incorporates the protective power of the juniper tree. The alcohol is mostly for a preservative effect, so any will do as long as it is at least 40 percent alcohol by volume. After adding the alcohol, pour the liquid into a mason jar or bottle that seals well. You can also of course make this without alcohol, but you will need to make sure to put the liquid in a jar or bottle that seals well and store it in the refrigerator for the duration of the ritual.

After your potion is made, you will now craft your ritual area. First, take the red piece of paper and draw a heart in each corner, facing outward. Then, in the center of the page, you are going to draw four more hearts, each with their pointed bases nearly touching the other. Starting with the top heart, write the letter D inside the shape, then continue clockwise with T, then Y, and finally P. Here's a picture of what you should have at the end:

Place this square on a table somewhere it won't be disturbed from the new to full moon. Place a bowl on top of the paper, then add a silver item. You can also use a silver bowl. Then place your bottled potion in the center of the bowl, making sure the silver item is touching the bottle; you can even place it on top of the jar lid. When you have everything set up, say, "As the moon grows, let my heart grow. As the moon grows, let my love grow. As the moon grows, let me grow closer and closer to my heart's true love. Let this potion grow and as the flowers that made it once blossomed, so let my love bloom."

Leave this ritual set up as it is until the next full moon. Repeat the phrase every day. On the full moon, repeat the phrase one more time, then drink your potion. It's believed that by the next full moon, you will have made contact with your true love.

If you left out the alcohol, you'll want to set up your ritual items inside the refrigerator to prevent the potion from spoiling before the full moon.

VARIATIONS: You can also set up the ritual exactly as described, but instead of making the potion beforehand, you can fill the bowl with yarrow flowers, or yarrow flowers and leaves, and bless them for the duration of the waxing moon. Then, on the full moon, make your infusion and drink it as in the ritual procedure.

BIBLE VERSE: Instead of the verbal charm listed in the spell section, you can recite Song of Solomon 7:11–13. "Come, my beloved, let us go forth into the fields, and lodge in the villages; let us go out early to the vineyards, and see whether the vines have budded, whether the grape blossoms have opened and the pomegranates are in bloom. There I will give you my love. The mandrakes give forth fragrance, and over our doors are all choice fruits, new as well as old, which I have laid up for you, O my beloved."

NOTES: The strange letters "DTYP" on the paper square were never fully explained to me by the informant who gave me this ritual. She said it was the abbreviation for an "ancient spell," as she called it, but the exact words had long been forgotten. She assured me, though, that even when not knowing what the letters meant, the ritual was still very effective.

RITUAL TO MEND A BROKEN HEART USING REDBUD FLOWERS

MAGICAL TIMING: New moon; Friday; Taurus or Cancer

INGREDIENTS:

- Bowl or measuring cup
- ¼ cup redbud flowers (*Cercis canadensis*)
- Honey
- Water

SPELL: This is a simple yet very effective spell to help mend a broken heart. Begin by heating a cup of water to boiling, then let stand for a minute to cool slightly. Put your water in a bowl or measuring cup. Next, add your quarter cup fresh or dried redbud flowers. Stir in a clockwise motion and, while stirring, repeat this verbal charm three times while watching the swirling water: "What has been broken, redbud mend. What has been shattered, redbud fix. What has been lost, redbud find. Mend my broken heart, redbud wise. Fix my shattered soul, redbud strong. Find the love I lost for myself, redbud kind."

After repeating the charm three times, strain your redbud tea into a cup, add a little honey to sweeten the spell, then drink and let redbud carry away the pain.

VARIATIONS: Other edible flowers can be used in place of redbud if these trees aren't available. These include violets, chamomile, roses, lavender, and other Ozark flowers like wild bergamot (*Monarda fistulosa*), beebalm (*Monarda didyma*), and spring beauty (*Claytonia virginica*). Perform the ritual in the exact same way as indicated under the spell section.

BIBLE VERSE: You can replace the verbal charm in the original spell with Psalm 23. "The Lord is my shepherd, I shall not want. He makes me lie down in green pastures; he leads me beside still waters; he restores my soul. He leads me in right paths for his name's sake. Even though I walk through the darkest valley, I fear no evil; for you are with me; your rod and your staff—they comfort me. You prepare a table before me in the presence of my enemies; you anoint my head with oil; my cup overflows. Surely goodness and mercy shall follow me all the days of my life, and I shall dwell in the house of the Lord my whole life long."

NOTES: Redbud flowers have a short life span on the tree and should be gathered as soon as they begin to bloom in the early spring. Once gathered, you can use them fresh, but I prefer to dry and bottle them for use throughout the year.

Chapter 4

MAGICAL CLEANSING

PLANET: Moon, Venus

ZODIAC: Cancer

DAY: Monday, Friday

COLOR: White, red

ITEMS:

- Brooms
- Eggs
- Knives
- Water

PLANTS:

- Horsemint (*Monarda bradburiana* or *M. fistulosa*)
- Mistletoe, American (*Phoradendron leucarpum*)
- Red cedar (*Juniperus virginiana*)
- Sassafras (*Sassafras albidum*)
- Sweet everlasting, Rabbit tobacco (*Pseudognaphalium obtusifolium*)
- Sweetgum (*Liquidambar styraciflua*)
- Tobacco (*Nicotiana tabacum* or *N. rustica*)

Rituals for magical cleansing and healing are among the top number of spells I've collected in my travels. We live in a very different time today, but in ages past, magic had to predominantly focus on three areas: health, the farm, and marriage. This was the winning combination to having a good life, according to old Ozarkers. One had to be in good health, with a thriving farm (even if it was just for your family's survival), and of course a spouse by your side to help you produce and maintain your lineage. Old rituals and spells mostly focused on growing or healing these areas or, in the case of marriage, the Ozarks have offered us a large number of divinatory methods for identifying one's future spouse.

Spells and methods for healing are vast and often vary from person to person. I myself have collected hundreds of wart charms and rituals, and I know for a fact that's only the tip of the iceberg. Other popular ailments that were much more threatening to our hillfolk ancestors include fevers, coughs, rheumatism, and a whole host of dermatological needs that often went under the name *tetter*. Coughs often went under the name of *croup* or *catarrh* and can range from minor congestion and lung trouble to much more serious illnesses like tuberculosis. In the old Ozarks, *rheumatism* often included rheumatoid arthritis, general pain and inflammation in the joints, and the rheumatic fever. Many charms and cures that once specifically targeted rheumatic fever, a much more serious illness for our elders than it is today, have instead turned into charms and cures for arthritis and joint pain amongst modern healers.

MAGICAL HEALING, PAST AND PRESENT

While of course these problems are still with us, healing amongst modern practitioners has tended to shift away from the chill-and-cough doctoring of our ancestors. Many healers today, myself included, first suggest the patient consult a doctor before any magical work is done. For me, this is because most minor ailments can easily be solved using the wonders of modern medicine. I've seen the focus of magic shifting over the years, even in rural areas.

Nowadays, modern witches are facing different sorts of problems than our ancestors had to deal with. For example, I see much more of what I call *soul work* being done to help individuals heal from trauma or work through all the existential funk the world throws at us on a daily basis. Magical cleanses, which in the past might have been for fevers and colds, now take on a different life as they heal fractured identities, anxiety, fear, body dysmorphia, and many more of what we might call "modern" illnesses. One healer

I met said something that has stuck with me for years now: "We've taken care of the body with medicine; now the spirit is crying out for healing."

In the old Ozarks, healing the body and spirit went hand in hand, but magic wasn't consulted on a daily basis like we often see today. You never had hillfolk going on weekend retreats to get back in touch with their souls and heal from mental and emotional trauma. Magic was often quick and focused on real-world, tangible illnesses that, if left to run their course, could mean—at best—not being able to put food on the table, or worse: death.

The only time lengthy rituals might be employed was in the case of serious magical illnesses or hexes. Often in these cases the healer would stay at their patient's home and help with household or farm chores, the idea being that if the affairs of the home were looked after, the patient could let themselves stop stressing and heal.

In other cases, a healer might have wanted to wait until the "signs were right," as they say, meaning putting off healing work until the moon phases and zodiac moon signs were correct. For many, this was and still is seen as unnecessary, especially in the case of illnesses or afflictions that needed to be addressed immediately. I myself work with the moon phases and zodiac signs as much as I can, but only with situations that can stand to wait for the "tokens," or signs, to be perfect.

CLEANSING THE BODY AND SOUL

Ritual cleanses often addressed those more serious magical illnesses and hexes. Cleansing in the Ozarks can fall into four categories: water, fire, smoke, and what I call *releasing*, which includes purgatives and emetics. As for a general overview of these methods, water cleansing involves either home baths using blessed water that was then poured over the head a certain number of times, or ritual bathing in a river or creek as a means to magically wash away hexes as well as physical illnesses.

Cleansing by fire involves using a flammable container, often made from paper or wax, to collect or suck out the hex or magical illness from a person's body. The container is then burned completely, often with certain accompanying verbal charms or prayers. In some cases, the smoke from this burning container might be observed by the healer to determine the effectiveness of the ritual.

Cleansing by smoke involves burning certain plant materials, commonly red cedar (*Juniperus virginiana*) or tobacco (*Nicotiana tabacum* or *N. rustica*), then using the smoke produced as a sort of extension of washing to cleanse a person or space of magical entities, curses, or illness. Many modern witches call this *smudging*, but I choose to use the old terms that are more culturally appropriate like *smoking, saining,* or *smooring. Smoking* is what I've commonly heard in the Ozarks, especially amongst older people or those not influenced by the New Age movement's obsession with smudging. *Saining* and *smooring* aren't heard in the Ozarks, but they come from the Scottish tradition of smoking the home with juniper branches as a method of cleansing. I like to use *smooring* as part of my practice to connect to my own Highlands ancestry.

Cleansing by releasing was once much more common in the old Ozarks, when purgatives and emetics were popular cures for everything from a fever to malaise. The appeal quickly ran out in the early twentieth century, but purgatives remained in cases of magical illness, in particular the ones considered deadly to the victim. Botanical decoctions would be administered, usually a strong purgative like Indian tobacco (*Lobelia inflata*), mayapple root (*Podophyllum peltatum*), or black gum bark (*Nyssa sylvatica*), along with verbal charms and prayers. Then the patient would purge under the healer's supervision until it was determined the curse had been removed. Often, releasing rituals like this went hand in hand with water cleansing, as the patient could purge into the river or creek and then be washed clean.

MISCELLANEOUS MAGICAL METHODS

Other methods of magical healing include such rituals as using containers like eggs as a means to suck out or remove certain illnesses or hexes. The container would then be destroyed, as in the method of cleansing with fire. Counting-down rituals were also quite popular at one time and are the source of many interesting verbal charms. In this method, the healer would reduce the illness or curse little by little until it was completely gone. The most common form of this ritual involves ten matches. The first match is lit with the phrase "Evil, you are not ten, you are nine!" The lit match is then thrown into a cup of water or into a creek. This continues down until the healer lights the last match and completely destroys the illness or curse with the words "Evil, you are not one, you are none!" Counting-down rituals can involve ingredients other than matches. They could be done with a loaf of bread, whereby little pieces would be taken from the loaf and thrown into a river until there's nothing left, or even a handful of pebbles, corn kernels, or beans thrown away—stone by stone, bean by bean—along with a hex.

I've included a good number of these quick spells and rituals for cleansing and healing in this chapter. Just because they are considered fast working doesn't mean they aren't powerful. For ages, the best spell to stop a bleeding wound has been a simple Bible verse, Ezekiel 16:6. "I passed by you, and saw you flailing about in your blood. As you lay in your blood, I said to you, 'Live!'" This was traditionally read three times over any wound. Simple charms like this one, or even catching illness in an egg or knots in a string, have been used and passed down not just because of their effectiveness, but because they can be applicable in so many different situations. While I've developed rituals in my own work that address issues related to personal identity, anger, and anxiety, many of the old methods can be repurposed for modern usage as well. For example, instead of catching hexes in a knot, you could repurpose this ritual method for stress, anger, or anything you might be dealing with. This is where the simplicity of Ozark folk methods becomes an advantage, as you are able to transform and adapt the method to any time and any ailment.

CONSULTING MEDICAL PROFESSIONALS

Before we begin the spell section of this chapter, I would like to note a few precautions to consider. Whenever we are dealing with sickness and the body, please consider consulting a medical professional first before looking to a magical method. That isn't to say that rituals and spell work have no place in the healing process, because they absolutely do. What I like to encourage is an integration of modern scientific methods with magical ones, where they can safely and effectively be merged.

Take this anecdote, for instance. In my travels, I once met a healer who was popular in her local rural community for being able to heal damn near anything from physical illnesses to what we might call magical ones, even though she preferred to use the term *soul sickness*. Her methods surprised me at first, having had so many interactions with Ozarkers who had a deep and ancient hatred for modern medicine. Before she worked for anyone, the healer would always ask if they'd been to the doctor first; if so, what their diagnosis was; and finally, if they'd been taking their medications as prescribed. If the answer to the first or last question was no, she would politely refuse service. Her clients all knew the routine, and when I met her she had three clients she was working with on a long-term basis. Her methods were simple and mostly used prayers and verbal charms derived from the Bible. Her main practice was praying over medical documents and prescription medication, which her clients would bring to her for her blessing. In the case of her regulars, they would leave her empty prescription bottles, which she kept lined up on top of an old Bible that had been passed down through her family. For this healer, and others like her in the Ozarks, healing the body and soul go hand in hand and shouldn't be separated. We need the prayers, rituals, and spells just as much as the medication some-times, and vice versa. The key, as with most things in the world, is maintaining a healthy balance between the two.

RITUAL TO CATCH A FEVER IN AN EGG

MAGICAL TIMING: Waning moon; Libra (opposite sign to Aries, which rules the head)

INGREDIENTS:

- 1 egg

SPELL: Take your egg and go to a swiftly flowing river or creek. For Ozarkers, the most auspicious cleansing rivers flow west, but any will do for these purposes. Blow three times over the egg then say these words three times: "When this egg again I see, fever then return to me!" After repeating the charm three times, throw the egg into the water, then turn around and leave without looking back.

VARIATIONS:

- If you can't go out to a river, you can also do this spell indoors. After blowing across the egg and reciting the verbal charm three times, as indicated in the spell section, crack the egg into the toilet and then flush. Dispose of the egg-shell in the trash.

- This ritual will also work for other illnesses and even hexes using the same suggested method, except with this verbal charm: "Shell, and white, and yolk, this evil choke, this sickness strangle and suck!" Repeat the charm three times, then pass the egg over your skin from head to toe before throwing it into a river or smashing it against a tree.

BIBLE VERSE: You can replace the verbal charm in the original spell with Mark 1:29–31. "As soon as they left the synagogue, they entered the house of Simon and Andrew, with James and John. Now Simon's mother-in-law was in bed with a fever, and they told him about her at once. He came and took her by the hand and lifted her up. Then the fever left her, and she began to serve them."

NOTES: As with many other Ozark spells, turning away and not looking back at the ritual site is a very important step in the process. This isn't to say you can never look back on that spot; that would be quite inconvenient if you used a toilet instead of the river. As I was once told, the point is to believe in the work and not obsess over the process.

Turning away and forgetting about the site allows you time to get distracted doing other things so the magic can work at its own pace.

RITUAL TO CLEANSE ILLNESSES AND HEXES WITH KNOTS

MAGICAL TIMING: Waning moon; zodiac moon day opposite where the illness is sitting

INGREDIENTS:

- String, white, whole spool

SPELL: Take some ordinary white string and wrap it loosely three times around the afflicted area (e.g., chest for coughs, forehead for fevers, etc.). Cut the string to this length. Make a knot toward one end but don't close it. As you hold the knot open, say, "Sickness be bound, for as long as the world shall last!" Then blow through the knot and close tight while you're blowing. Repeat this process along the string for a total of seven knots. Once finished, tie the string around your right wrist and wear it until it naturally falls off.

VARIATIONS:

- Instead of tying the string around your wrist, you can also hang it in the branches of a witch tree. See the section on witch trees in chapter 1 for a list of common species. Typically, healers will use pawpaw (*Asimina triloba*) or sassafras (*Sassafras albidum*) trees.

- You can also use this verbal charm instead of the one provided in the spell section. First, say these words while holding the string: "This sickness, this evil, I gather piece by piece and blow it away!" Next, make a knot on the left end of the string, but don't close it completely. After each line of the spell, blow through an open knot, then finish by pulling the knot closed and continuing with the next one in line. In the end, you should have nine knots for the nine lines of the spell:

  One, a piece into a mighty rock,
  Two, a piece into the pine tops,
  Three, a piece into the rushing river,
  Four, a piece into the deep lake,
  Five, a piece into the sassafras tree,
  Six, a piece into the plum pit,
  Seven, a piece into the running elk,

> Eight, a piece into the unmovable earth,
>
> Nine, a piece into the shining sun!

BIBLE VERSE: You can replace the verbal charm in the original spell with Psalm 51:7. "Purge me with hyssop, and I shall be clean; wash me, and I shall be whiter than snow."

NOTES: It might seem troublesome to have to wear the string until it falls off, but the theory behind this is that not only are you healing the illness at hand, but you are also helping prevent or ward off the illness from returning through the use of the prayers that were magically "caught" in the knots.

A CHARM BAG FOR GOOD HEALTH

MAGICAL TIMING: New moon to full moon; Cancer

INGREDIENTS:

- Camphor essential oil or gin
- Silver bowl or silver item
- Small cloth bag with drawstring top, white
- String, white or red, 3 1-foot lengths

3 BRANCHES (SMALL PIECE):

- Elderberry (*Sambucus nigra* or *S. canadensis*)
- Spicebush (*Lindera benzoin*)
- Witch hazel (*Hamamelis virginiana* or *H. vernalis*, "Ozark witch hazel")

3 LEAVES:

- Common dittany, stone mint (*Cunila origanoides*)
- Horsemint (*Monarda bradburiana* or *M. fistulosa*, "wild bergamot")
- Rabbit tobacco (*Pseudognaphalium obtusifolium*)

3 ROOTS (SMALL PIECE):

- Burdock (*Arctium lappa*)
- Dandelion (*Taraxacum officinale*)
- Sassafras (*Sassafras albidum*)

SPELL: This amulet combines nine species of plants in total: three branches, three leaves, and three roots. Each of these plants has a long history of use both medicinally and magically, but when combined in such a way as this, the resulting amulet is quite potent.

- The branches and leaves should be harvested on the full moon, when the plant's energy has been drawn into the aerial portions of the plant. Taurus or Cancer are the best moon days for this, and second best are any earth or water sign days.

- Roots should be harvested on the new moon, when the plant's energy has retreated downward. Again, choose a new moon in Taurus or Cancer, or any earth/water sign days.

- Healing plants are generally harvested at nighttime or in the early morning, as it's believed that the sun can reduce the plant's energies.

Once you have all your plants gathered, you can begin assembling your charm bag. Traditionally, amulets are created on the new moon, then allowed to grow in their magic until the full moon, when they are "sealed."

On the new moon, begin by tying your roots and branches in their own separate bundles using white or red string. Next, add your bundles to a small cloth bag with a drawstring top, but don't tie the top closed yet. Once assembled, place the bag in a silver bowl, or a regular bowl with a silver item placed alongside the bag, so that they are touching. Blow three times over the bag, each time visualizing the roots, branches, and leaves in the bag beginning to come to life and grow. Repeat this blowing action and visualization every day until the full moon.

On the full moon, repeat the blowing and visualization, this time seeing the bag completely engulfed in light and the leaves, roots, and branches full of sap and energy. Pull the top of the bag closed and seal with three knots. Carry this bag with you as a ward against illnesses, hexes, and anything that would come against you. Recharge every full and new moon using three drops of camphor essential oil or gin.

VARIATIONS: These traditional ingredients are offered as a suggestion of what one recipe might call for, but perhaps you have a plant ally or allies you like to work with instead. You can always replace one or more of the leaves, branches, and roots with plant species that are more meaningful or plentiful for you.

BIBLE VERSE: Along with the three breaths in the original spell, you can also repeat Revelation 22:1–2. "Then the angel showed me the river of the water of life, bright as crystal, flowing from the throne of God and of the Lamb through the middle of the street of the city. On either side of the river is the tree of life with its twelve kinds of fruit, producing its fruit each month; and the leaves of the tree are for the healing of the nations."

NOTES: There are countless recipes for charm bags in the Ozarks, most of which act as wards against either specific ailments or sickness in general. Usually, all charm bags incorporate sacred numbers like three, seven, nine, or twelve when it comes to figuring up the amount and types of ingredients they may include. Amulets hardly ever just have one ingredient, although in the old days, the most popular charm bag for warding off sickness and evil was simply a bag filled with asafetida (*Ferula assa-foetida*), also called *asafetidy, asafedy,* or *devil's dung* in the Ozarks. Asafetida is a truly horrible-smelling plant used in both Old and New World folk magic as a ward against all sorts of evil entities and illnesses. I've met many old-timers who have shared memories of being forced to carry bags of the stinking plant around their necks as children.

RITUAL TO PASS THROUGH A HOOP OF STRING FOR HEALING

MAGICAL TIMING: Waning moon; Monday or Friday; Cancer

INGREDIENTS:

- String, white or red, whole spool

SPELL: Measure a length of string from your head to toes plus shoulder to shoulder, then cut this length from the spool. Tie the two ends of the string together to form a large hoop. Pass this hoop from head to toe, then pull it out from underneath your feet. Repeat this three times while saying this verbal charm each time: "Evil, sickness, and blight, left behind by this might! This power, this string, this golden ring!"

After the third time, take the string and tie it in the branches of a strong oak tree or burn it to ash on a fire of oak wood.

VARIATIONS: In one interesting variation that was given to me, you can instead use a doorway to perform this spell. First, you will want a cleansing liquid of some kind. The healer who gave me this variation used ordinary all-purpose kitchen cleaner, but you can also use diluted colognes or perfumes like Florida Water or a mixture of one cup unflavored vodka/gin and twelve drops of camphor essential oil in a spray bottle.

While standing inside your house facing the open doorway, repeat the verbal charm three times, replacing the word *string* with *gate*. After the third time, step through the doorway. Immediately spray down the frame of the door with your cleaner or cleansing spray, then wipe with rags or a towel. Once finished, you can reenter the house.

While you can use any open doorway, using one that exits your house has the added symbolic benefit of leaving the sickness or hex behind outside.

BIBLE VERSE: You can replace the verbal charm in the original spell with Psalm 51:6–9. "You desire truth in the inward being; therefore teach me wisdom in my secret heart. Purge me with hyssop, and I shall be clean; wash me, and I shall be whiter than snow. Let me hear joy and gladness; let the bones that you have crushed rejoice. Hide your face from my sins, and blot out all my iniquities."

NOTES: This ritual makes use of an ancient belief in the curative and magical powers of completely closed rings and arches. For example, in the Ozarks, hole stones, hole roots, and even naturally occurring arches like those made from blackberry or raspberry canes have been used by healers and witches for centuries. Many of these beliefs would have been brought with families from across Europe, where similar traditions are still in place today. Hole stones, also known as hag stones or adder stones, as well as roots with naturally occurring holes, have predominantly been used as tools for blessing healing waters and medicines. In these rituals, the liquid would be poured through the hole and collected in a container on the other side. This was seen as passing through the otherworld, where blessings and magical energy could be caught and brought back into our world.

Blackberry and raspberry canes also have a long history of use in the Ozarks. These plants have the unique quality of being able to take root at both ends of the cane, forming bramble arches. These gateways were once seen as holding great supernatural power and were used much like the hoop of string to remove illness and curses. In this ritual, a person would crawl through the arch in a certain direction (usually to the east if possible) then stand, walk back around, and repeat the movement three times in total. It was believed the illness or curse would get caught on the blackberry's prickly cane and be left behind in the forest.

RITUAL TO COLLECT ILLNESSES AND HEXES IN A GLASS OF WATER

MAGICAL TIMING: Waning moon; Monday; Cancer

INGREDIENTS:

- Glass or cup of water

SPELL: An old Ozark method for snatching up any illness or hex involves a simple glass of water and a verbal charm. First, place a glass of fresh water at the head of your bed just before you go to sleep. Repeat this verbal charm three times, blowing once across the water after each recitation: "Water, water! As the river carries leaves away, carry this sickness away! As the river carries leaves away, carry this evil away! As the river carries leaves away, carry this darkness away! Water, water! Flow into the east. Flow back up the mountain."

The next morning, you can either pour the water into the toilet and flush, or you can take the water and pour it into a creek or river, the idea being that the sickness or hex that was collected is then carried off by this action.

VARIATIONS:

- For an acute illness, no specific timing is needed. For something more chronic, however, you can repeat this every night from the full to new moon.

- I've met several healers who use this as a daily cleansing ritual, especially those who have clients coming inside their homes. Glasses of water can also be blessed using the verbal charm provided in the spell section and then left around the house to suck up any bad energies or entities that might be hanging around. The water is then disposed of once it has collected whatever might have been present. Often certain "tokens" are looked for, like cloudiness of the water, as a sign that the ritual was successful.

BIBLE VERSE: You can replace the verbal charm in the original spell with Revelation 7:16–17. "They will hunger no more, and thirst no more; the sun will not strike them, nor any scorching heat; for the Lamb at the center of the throne will be their shepherd, and he will guide them to springs of the water of life, and God will wipe away every tear from their eyes."

NOTES: There's a related Ozark practice of keeping a bowl of water underneath the bed of someone with a fever or severe illness. I've even heard anecdotes of this practice being used to help people with bad sunburns or heat exhaustion. The magic is derived from a sympathetic connection between the heat inside the person's body and the cool water that doesn't even need to come into contact with the person in order to abate the illness. I've asked a few older healers about this practice, and they told me the water was also used as a container. Knowledge of the real meaning behind this practice was often lost on ordinary onlookers, many of whom would later report much simpler interpretations of the practice, such as that the water somehow cooled the bed above it.

RITUAL TO CLEANSE USING MATCHES

MAGICAL TIMING: Waning moon; Monday or Friday; Cancer

INGREDIENTS:

- 10 matches, with box for striking
- Small cup or bowl of water

SPELL: This ritual can be performed anywhere, but I prefer working outside. Take a small bowl or cup of water and ten matches with you. It's easiest if you have a table to work on while you are outside. Face west while working this ritual. In Ozark cosmology, east is considered the direction of blessing whereas west is considered the land where all sickness and evil resides. In this ritual, you are facing west because you want to send whatever illness or curse you're removing back in that direction. Likewise, the ritual remains are disposed of toward the west for this same reason. The bowl of water should be in front of you on the table and the matches with box for striking should be next to it. This is a counting-down ritual, so you will be lighting a match, saying some words, then tossing it into the bowl. The verbal charm used goes like this:

> Evil, I reduce you for (FIRST MIDDLE LAST)!
> Sickness, you are not ten, you are nine.
> You are not nine, you are eight.
> You are not eight, you are seven.
> You are not seven, you are six.
> You are not six, you are five.
> You are not five, you are four.
> You are not four, you are three.

You are not three, you are two.
You are not two, you are one.
You are not one, you are none!

As each initial number is named, strike a match, let the flame build, then toss or drop it into the water so that it is extinguished. At the end of the ritual, all ten matches should have been lit and then tossed into the water. Once finished, take the bowl of water with the matches and toss the contents toward the west, either onto an oak tree or onto one of the witch trees listed in chapter 1.

VARIATIONS: Instead of tossing the water onto a tree, there are several other traditional ways of disposing of the ritual remains. You could also pour the water and matches into a hole at the base of a witch tree, then replace the dirt. You could face west and toss the water and matches into a river or creek. You could also stand in the middle of a four-way crossroads and toss the water and matches over your left shoulder, then return home without looking back.

BIBLE VERSE: None

NOTES: Counting-down rituals are common ways of removing sickness and hexes in Ozarks folk practice. There are countless methods to achieve this goal; these rituals don't have to be done with matches. Anything that can be "reduced" can be used. Other common items used in counting-down rituals include loaves of bread, beans, corn kernels, small pebbles, carved sticks, and even coins like pennies.

RITUAL TO CLEANSE USING A BATH

MAGICAL TIMING: Waning moon; Monday or Friday; Cancer; dawn

INGREDIENTS:

- Clean clothes
- Pinch of salt
- Pitcher of water
- Small bowl or coffee mug
- Towel

PLANTS (OPTIONAL):

- Common dittany, "stone mint" (*Cunila origanoides*)

- Horsemint (*Monarda bradburiana* or *M. fistulosa*)

- Lemon balm (*Melissa officinalis*)

- Mint (*Mentha* spp. cultivated or *Pycnanthemum* spp., "mountain mint")

- Rabbit tobacco (*Pseudognaphalium obtusifolium*)

SPELL: Preparing a cleansing bath at home can be as simple as filling a plastic or glass pitcher full of warm water and adding a pinch of salt. You can also add some of the plants listed under the optional plants section in the ingredients list. In that case, you will want to use hot water and let the plants steep for around ten minutes before straining the foliage and collecting the water back into the pitcher.

It should be noted here that an Ozark cleansing bath is not a soak in the tub like we're used to today. This is a "quick cleanse," as they say, meant to wash away any illness or hex fast. Also, cleansing by water is traditionally performed just before dawn to act as a symbolic rebirth for the person being cleansed.

Once you've got your water (either with or without the plants), take your pitcher to your bath/shower or outside. Bring a towel and a small bowl or coffee mug with you. Once in the shower or outside, disrobe. Place the bowl or mug at your feet. Repeat this verbal charm over the water three times: "Water pure and clean, carry this evil with your current! Carry it far away from me! Carry it into the west where all evil lives! Let it stay there until the world is destroyed!" After you've finished, pour the water from the pitcher over your head three times. By the end of the third pour, all of the water should be gone.

Next, dry off and put on some clean clothes, then take the bowl or mug you placed at your feet, which should now have some water in it, and pour the water onto the roots of an oak tree or a witch tree. You can also pour the water into a river or creek.

VARIATIONS: The most common variation on this ritual is taking a cleansing bath in a river or creek. In this case, no pitcher, salt, or plants are needed. Face west while standing in the creek or river, then dunk yourself fully under the water three times. Repeat the verbal charm listed in the spell section before going under the water each time.

BIBLE VERSE:

- Psalm 51:7. "Purge me with hyssop, and I shall be clean: wash me, and I shall be whiter than snow."

- If you are using a river to cleanse with, you can recite Revelation 22:1–2 three times while in the water. After each recitation, dunk yourself underneath the water. "Then the angel showed me the river of the water of life, bright as crystal, flowing from the throne of God and of the Lamb through the middle of the street of the city. On either side of the river is the tree of life with its twelve kinds of fruit, producing its fruit each month; and the leaves of the tree are for the healing of the nations."

NOTES: In many of the older rituals, the person who was being cleansed would be stripped naked and their old clothes, thought to also contain the illness or curse, would be burned. After the bath, the afflicted individual, now cleansed by the water, would be given a new set of clothes as an extension of this symbolic rebirth. In modern variations, your old clothes can be cleansed of any residual illness or hexes by simply washing them with ordinary laundry detergent and a pinch of salt. You can also repeat the verbal charm or Bible verses above over this water as well.

RITUAL TO REMOVE THE EVIL EYE

MAGICAL TIMING: Waning moon; Monday or Friday; Cancer or Libra

INGREDIENTS:

- 7 charcoal briquettes, with metal tongs
- 7 cloves of garlic
- Lighter or matches
- Metal stockpot or large cooking pot
- Red cedar leaves, fresh or dried (*Juniperus virginiana*)
- Red cedar stick, 2 feet
- Yarrow flowers, fresh or dried (*Achillea millefolium*)

CAUTIONS: Because of the charcoal and red cedar used in this ritual, the water created should be for external use only.

SPELL: First, fill your stockpot with water. This can be ordinary tap water or spring water, whichever is available to you. Add a handful of red cedar leaves, seven cloves of garlic, and a handful of yarrow flowers. After this, heat up seven charcoal briquettes in a heat-safe grill or firepit until they are completely hot. Some charcoal briquettes already contain lighter fluid and only need to be lit using matches or a lighter. Depending upon the charcoal you use, you might need to add some lighter fluid to get the briquettes started. As the coals heat, blow over them three times, saying these words each time you blow: "Seven crows pluck out seven evil eyes!"

Once the coals are hot, drop them into the pot one at a time. Stir the mixture with a red cedar stick while saying, "An evil eye looked at you, may they be snuffed out. May they be poked and dug out. Seven times with a crow's beak! Seven times with a cedar stick! Seven times with a hot coal!"

Once the liquid has cooled, strain out the solids. Finish by washing your hands in the water and then sprinkling the water over your left and right shoulder using the fingers of your right hand, three times on each side. You can dispose of the rest of the water as well as the solids that were strained off at the roots of a strong oak tree.

VARIATIONS: A common variation is to combine this ritual with a counting-down spell using matches. In this case, you would leave out the charcoal, but all other elements would stay the same. At the moment in the ritual where you would add the hot coals, instead repeat the counting-down ritual detailed in the spell "Ritual to Cleanse Using Matches." Extinguish each match into the pot of water and herbs. Once finished, let cool and strain off the liquid, then wash your hands using this water.

BIBLE VERSE: Instead of the verbal charms used in the beginning and while stirring, you can use Numbers 21:18 both times. "'Spring up, O well!—Sing to it!—the well that the leaders sank, that the nobles of the people dug, with the scepter, with the staff.'"

NOTES:

- The evil eye is a cross-cultural phenomenon that has popped up across the world in many different forms. Not all Ozarkers I've met believe in the evil eye. Many others do, but under different names like "the eye" or "wasting." Generally speaking, this magical illness is caused by jealousy from others and isn't necessarily any sort of malicious hex. For this reason, many traditional Ozarkers are very secretive when it comes to announcing their own successes for fear that by spreading their successes around to too many people, someone might become jealous of them and thereby send them "the eye." This also applies to newborns—and children in general—within the family. At one time, there was a belief that a newborn should spend the first six to eight months in complete seclusion at home with the immediate family before anyone could see it. This was to protect the child from deadly illnesses that might result from any jealous glances. Along these same lines, traditional Ozarkers often don't pay babies and children as many compliments as city folk do. Receiving too many compliments is said to risk having "the eye" placed on you, and I've met a few old-timers who had a falling out with friends and family members for complimenting their child too much.

- A couple different informants told me to always use Libra when healing the evil eye. This connects back to the "Man of Signs," or the Zodiac Man diagram. According to this theory, the eyes are associated with Aries; therefore, curses and illnesses located in the eyes, including the evil eye, should be cured in the opposite sign, Libra.

- Traditionally in the Ozarks, the water for this ritual would be collected from a creek or river that flows east. Since east is considered the direction of blessing, this water was seen as being naturally charged by magical energies.

RITUAL TO TIE HEXES TO A TREE

MAGICAL TIMING: Waning moon; new moon; Monday or Friday; Cancer

INGREDIENTS:

- String, red, whole spool

SPELL: In the Ozarks, a simple and popular method for removing illness and curses is by tying, or binding, them to a tree. This spell works best with a partner.

Go out to a witch tree of any variety listed in chapter 1. If you are the one who is hexed, put your back firmly against the bark of the tree. Have your partner place their hands on either side of your head and repeat this verbal charm: "What I tie here, I leave here, in the name of all that is good and holy in the world. I tie up this evil for (FIRST MIDDLE LAST) that they might be healed and live a long and happy life." The name should be the full name of the one who is hexed.

After this, have your partner wrap string around your chest and the tree trunk three times. Make the string tight enough that it doesn't fall away easily but loose enough for you to be able to wiggle out. After these three rounds, lower yourself down and out of the string. With this loop still around the tree trunk, tie it tight, knotting it three times. Repeat this phrase while you are tying: "What I tie here, I leave here!"

Finish the spell by walking away with your partner without looking back.

VARIATIONS: I've also heard of people using fence posts and telephone poles in tying rituals like this one. One old-timer I met swore the best way to cure chills and fever was to tie them to a fence post made from black locust wood (*Robinia pseudoacacia*), a common building material in the rural Ozarks. Apart from using a fence post instead of a tree, he used nearly the same ritual as detailed in the spell section, but he simplified the initial verbal charm to just "What I tie here, I leave here!"

BIBLE VERSE: None

NOTES: Tying rites like this one were once very popular amongst Ozark healers for curing all sorts of different ailments and illnesses. The informant who gave me this ritual process still used this method frequently for herself and her clients. I asked if the witch trees ever suffered because of all the sickness, disease, and curses people were always leaving behind in their bark and roots and she said that no, the witch trees were able to survive because they were witch trees. She seemed to imply with her words that ordinary trees might not be able to handle such responsibility.

CRAFTING A HEALING BLADE FROM MISTLETOE

MAGICAL TIMING: Full moon; Sunday; Leo

INGREDIENTS:

- Heat-safe bowl/plate or incense burner
- Knife for carving
- Lighter or matches
- 1 mistletoe branch, 1 foot (*Phoradendron leucarpum* or *Viscum album*, "European mistletoe")
- Red cedar leaves, fresh or dried (*Juniperus virginiana*)

CAUTIONS: While European mistletoe (*Viscum album*) was traditionally used internally by herbalists, *this species is very rare in the US*. American mistletoe (*Phoradendron leucarpum*) can be toxic if ingested, especially the berries. Do not consume any part of the plant. Smoke from burning American mistletoe can also irritate the lungs and esophagus. Be sure to wear gloves when gathering and working with the fresh foliage. Dried mistletoe is relatively inert, but the fresh sap can cause contact dermatitis where it comes into contact with the skin.

SPELL: Gather your mistletoe on the Winter Solstice to add to the knife's magical potency. On the full moon, preferably in Leo as mistletoe is associated with the sun, carve away any excess branches or leaves on your mistletoe until you have a good-sized, straight rod from which will come the knife. This is often difficult to accomplish! Trust me on this. You might have to do a lot of searching before you find a bundle of mistletoe large enough to yield the perfect branch.

Once you've got your mistletoe rod, take your carving knife and slide it from the middle of the branch to the end, shaving off a good piece of the wood. Flip the branch over and repeat on the other side. Continue this whittling action until you form the flat, tapered blade of your knife. Make sure you leave enough room for your handle! This is only a symbolic knife, so if your blade doesn't come out perfect, don't worry. You can carve as much or as little as you like.

When you're finished carving, light some red cedar boughs and let the smoke waft over the mistletoe knife. Repeat this verbal charm three times while continuing to hold the knife in the smoke: "Green in the tree, blade in my hand. Sun in the tree, sun in my hand. I hold this knife; I hold this light. To cut, to cleave, to sever, and stab."

Traditionally, magical blades like this would be wrapped in a piece of cloth, leather, or even a handkerchief to keep it secret. Ritual knives like these were not display items in the home; they were only ever taken out of their hiding place for use during magical work.

VARIATIONS: If you don't want to carve the mistletoe wood, make a wand instead! Clear away any stray branches or leaves until you are left with a rod, as long as you want. Follow the same procedure as in the spell section by smoking the wand and repeating the verbal charm three times.

BIBLE VERSE: You can replace the verbal charm in the original spell with Revelation 1:16. "In his right hand he held seven stars, and from his mouth came a sharp, two-edged sword, and his face was like the sun shining with full force."

NOTES: Mistletoe is one of the forgotten plants of healing and magic in the Ozarks. In the old days, it was used in rituals for everything from love magic, to healing, to keeping witches away from your livestock. Today, few people know about its benefits apart from the custom of hanging mistletoe in the house from the Winter Solstice until Twelfth Night, or Old Christmas, as a ward of protection and good luck. Mistletoe has ancient connections to Pan-European folk traditions, many of which are direct ancestors of our Ozark folkways. As I was taught, mistletoe is associated with light and the sun, so it is always gathered on the Winter Solstice as a means of trapping and utilizing the last remaining sunlight, stored and heightened specifically in mistletoe, before the darkening of the year. For this reason, tools fashioned from mistletoe are particularly potent in work for healing and against the forces of evil.

RITUAL TO CLEANSE YOUR HOME

MAGICAL TIMING: New moon; Monday or Friday; Taurus or Cancer

INGREDIENTS:

- Cast-iron skillet or incense burner
- Incense charcoal, with metal tongs
- Lighter or matches
- Red cedar leaves and/or berries, fresh or dried (*Juniperus virginiana*)

SPELL: This is a very simple but powerful method for cleansing your home using red cedar smoke. While there are many other plants that have been used for this ritual, some of which are mentioned in the variations section, red cedar is most beloved by the Ozark people and has long been used in a variety of cleansing rites. Harvest your red cedar on the full moon, preferably in Cancer. Let it dry out for a complete moon cycle plus the following waning moon.

On the next new moon, light your charcoal by holding it in the flame from a lighter or matches, making sure to use metal tongs as the coal will get hot quickly. Place it either in an incense burner or the traditional Ozark tool for this kind of work, a cast-iron skillet. Whatever you use, make sure it is heatproof and has a handle.

Stand inside your house facing your front door. Add some of your red cedar to the coal and let it begin to smoke. Say these words while still facing the door: "Smoke cleanse, smoke bless, smoke purify. Three white flames come down off the mountain. One flame to heal, one flame to cleanse, and one flame to drive back all evil. Fires burn up any curses! Fires burn up any sickness! Fires burn up any evil! Let this smoke be a shield; let it be strong armor."

Carry this smoke through your entire house in a counterclockwise circle three times, starting and ending at the front door. Clockwise is seen as the direction of adding, growing, or blessing, whereas counterclockwise is traditionally used in cleansing rites because it is the direction of removal. Make sure you pass through every room, every hallway, and every closet. Try to keep to the counterclockwise direction if you can, but make sure you always begin and end at the front door.

After three passes, walk out the front door carrying your smoking skillet or incense burner and make three clockwise circles in front of the doorway. Let the red cedar continue to smolder. Then, once the ash has cooled completely, sprinkle at the base of an oak tree or throw into a moving body of water. The skillet or incense burner should be cleansed using salt water before it is brought back into the house.

VARIATIONS:

- If you're sensitive to smoke, try out an herbal spray instead. They're easy to craft and work just as well as smoking in cleansing both the inside and outside of your home. To make a simple red cedar cleanse, first make a tincture or infusion of some red cedar leaves and berries. For the infusion, let the red cedar steep in just-boiled water (not boiling) until it comes to room temperature. You can use this straight in a spray bottle, or you can dilute it if the smell is too strong. Use the same cleansing method as listed in the spell section, just replace the smoke with your spray, which you will spritz into the air every few feet as you walk through the rooms of your home. I also like to make a red cedar tincture by leaving about a cup of mixed leaves and berries to soak in a quart-sized mason jar of vodka for about a month. Strain off the liquid and bottle. You can fortify this with some juniper essential oil.

- In addition to red cedar, tobacco has also been traditionally used in the Ozarks as a cleansing plant, both inside and outside the home. Instead of using a skillet or other dish for burning the plant, a pipe or homemade cigarette would be the preferred method for smoking. In the simplest ritual, a healer might smoke the outside (or inside) of the house using a pipe of tobacco by starting at the front door and then making three counterclockwise circles around the entire house—and sometimes the entire property itself. The ritual concludes back at the front door, where the healer usually taps out the remaining contents of their pipe on the ground to the right of the door. There are a few theories behind this action; the most common says the remaining tobacco helps protect the front door from any evil that might want to sneak back inside. Another theory says that the remaining tobacco is food for any spirits that might be hanging around the house as a sort of payment for their services in helping to protect the family.

- Sweetgum (*Liquidambar styraciflua*) bark or leaves can also be used on its own for cleansing, or it can be used with other plants mentioned in this section for cleansing smoke. You can also collect the sticky sap or gum of the tree and use it as a powerful and fragrant incense.

- A less savory—but very effective—smoke fumigation has traditionally been asafetida (*Ferula assa-foetida*), also mentioned in "A Charm Bag for Good Health." Asafetida is a noxious-smelling plant whose odor is one of the most effective repellents for all sickness, curses, and evil in general. I don't recommend using asafetida as a smoke inside your home unless the circumstances are dire; it's a stench that will linger despite all your best efforts. Using it outside is easier, but make sure to cover your face as the smoke can irritate your lungs and throat. You can perform this smoke cleanse by circling the outside of your house three times, counterclockwise, starting and ending at the front door. Once finished, let the coal cool completely, then toss the ash and remaining asafetida into a river or creek.

BIBLE VERSE: You can replace the verbal charm in the original spell with Psalm 51:6–9. "You desire truth in the inward being; therefore teach me wisdom in my secret heart. Purge me with hyssop, and I shall be clean; wash me, and I shall be whiter than snow. Let me hear joy and gladness; let the bones that you have crushed rejoice. Hide your face from my sins, and blot out all my iniquities."

NOTES: Many of our smoke cleansing traditions have come from Old World variations, including the Scottish Highlands practice of using juniper smoke inside the home to clear out any sickness or evil. This seems to be a direct transplant to the Ozarks, where we use our very own juniper variety, red cedar (*Juniperus virginiana*). Using smoke as a method of cleansing is by no means specific to one culture, but I try to avoid using the term *smudging*, as I mentioned in the introduction to this chapter, choosing instead terms like *smoking* or *suffumigation*, or traditional Scottish terms like *smooring* and *saining*, to connect back to my own Highland ancestors.

Using tobacco smoke as a cleansing plant was inherited at least in part from interactions with Indigenous people of the Southeast, while proto-Ozarkers were still in their Appalachian motherland. To what extent these rituals were copied over by hillfolk isn't really understood still. It's most likely that while hillfolk might have incorporated the use of tobacco in their own predominantly European–based rituals, the original Indigenous significance would have been entirely lost to them.

PROTECTION

PLANET: Mars, Sun

ZODIAC: Aries, Taurus (for the home), Scorpio

DAY: Sunday, Tuesday, Friday (Taurus)

COLOR: Blue, red

ITEMS:

- Buckeye
- Claws: bear, cougar, buzzard, hawk, owl
- Hole stone (hag stone, adder stone)
- Nails and needles
- Silver items: dimes, rings, chains
- Teeth: coyote, wolf, bear, rattlesnake fangs
- Thorns: honey locust (*Gleditsia triacanthos*), pear tree

PLANTS:

- Asafetida (*Ferula assa-foetida*)
- Buckeye nut (*Aesculus glabra*)
- Camphor resin or oil (*Cinnamomum camphora*)
- Honey locust (*Gleditsia triacanthos*)
- Red cedar (*Juniperus virginiana*)

- Sweetgum (*Liquidambar styraciflua*)
- Solomon's seal root (*Polygonatum* spp.)
- Yarrow (*Achillea millefolium*)

Working for magical protection has meant many things for Ozark hillfolk. In the old days, protection work extended not only to the very real and present dangers of the wilderness, but also to deadly sicknesses and magical forces like the figure of the witch, who was often considered just as real and dangerous as any physical attacker or contagion. As I mentioned in the introduction, up until more modern years, magical acts in the Ozarks were always associated with evil and witchcraft. Healers used specific language, a high position in the community, and religious piety to protect themselves from being accused of witchcraft, despite oftentimes working with eerily similar processes and powers. The witch was then always someone on the fringes of society, and likely a person who was already marginalized in one way or another, be it because of age, marital status, sexual or gender identity, disability, or any of the other hundreds of reasons a more conservative, rural community might come up with to blame all their problems on one person.

Work for magical protection was used by magical practitioners and on behalf of the community at large to shield and guard against these ever-present forces of evil. Rituals for protection were usually always reactionary, not preventative. For example, let's say someone in town came down with a terrible sickness that stumped even the local country doctor. A healer with the gift was brought in to determine if a curse had been thrown. Through specific divination methods, the healer then determined that the illness was actually a curse sent by the local witch, who was usually also a person known by the community. The healer cleansed the person of the hex, then gave them (as well as sometimes the wider community) certain methods of protection to help prevent the effects of another curse. Meanwhile, the healer worked in private to reduce the power of the so-called witch, or the healer worked some kind of retribution ritual to return the curse to sender. The key idea to note here is that in a more traditional practice, the best form of personal protection was oftentimes getting rid of the person or entity who meant you harm. We work in a better way today, in my humble opinion.

WITCHES OF LORE AND REALITY

Modern practitioners in the Ozarks, even those in more rural areas, have mostly thrown out the old vision of the witch. That's certainly not to say that fear surrounding witch covens and the general "satanic panic" that sprung up in the '80s and '90s aren't still features of many more conservative communities. Preachers across the Ozarks still warn about the "slippery slope" that leads to witchcraft and demon worship from their pulpits every Sunday. But the situation is very different when it comes to the opinions of healers and magical practitioners *themselves*—you know, the ones who, in the old days, would have constantly feared being accused of witchcraft. While many of these modern practitioners and healers might still live in communities where they need to keep their gifts and work hidden from spying eyes, for the majority today the word *witch* means something very different than it used to.

This was one area that I really wanted to dig deep into while traveling across the Ozarks collecting information. Growing up as a part of a more conservative Christian church in the '90s, I occasionally had to sit through sermons about the dangers of the Harry Potter book series or popular television shows like *Sabrina the Teenage Witch*. As I got older, I formed very different opinions the more I read into the panic of the '80s and '90s surrounding so-called "satanism" and witchcraft. When I headed out into the hills and hollers, one question I took with me was "How has the view of witches changed since Vance Randolph first published *Ozark Magic and Folklore?*" Were people still scared of the local witch? And were healers still targeting witches as a part of their practice?

What I've come to find is that the vision of magical illness and protection work have greatly changed amongst practitioners and healers in the Ozarks. Whereas in the old days, a healer might view an actual local individual as a witch who cursed their client, today this has become something completely different. The source for curses, hexes, and other magical illnesses has been relocated away from the community for the most part. Instead of a healer returning a hex to a local widow, for instance, they might instead target the very idea of evil itself; "evil sent this thing, and to evil I send it back," as part of one verbal charm I collected goes. Works for magical protection then seek to protect against this formless, more spiritual idea of evil in the world, thereby almost completely removing the idea of the localized witch.

In some cases, traditional healers today will still target a witch in their cleansing and protection work, but what I've found is that it's almost never an actual person. One healer sent his curses back to "Witch Mountain," a tall bluff not too far from his community. This was a local hotspot for supernatural activity of the evil variety. Another healer always targeted the "witch of the woods" in their prayers and verbal charms. I asked if this was a real person or a more supernatural vision of the witch and he just replied, "Of course they're real!" When I asked their name, the healer assured me that while the witch was real—and local people had even seen her a few times—he believed she was actually a ghost who had kept her power and was still able to throw hexes. This is a giant leap from targeting a real member of the community to be on the receiving end of social ostracization and unwarranted violence.

PROTECTION IN A MODERN WORLD

Protection magic in general has changed greatly over the years. Work amongst practitioners today mostly focuses on preventing harm rather than just reacting to whatever terrible thing might happen after the fact. Amulets as well as rituals tend to target real-world enemies or this cosmic idea of evil rather than the stereotypical witch of the past. Many of the same protective plants, tools, and other magical items have carried over from the old Ozarks into more modern rituals like the ones in this chapter. Protective items include more well-known examples like the buckeye nut, hole stone, and items made out of silver. Less common personal talismans come from the animal kingdom and include claws and teeth, especially from predators like wolves, coyotes, and bears. Talons from certain birds of prey like hawks, owls, and even the eagle are also included in this category. These items are sometimes carried in the pocket or even worn as a necklace for magical protection. This forms a sympathetic connection for the holder where the claws and teeth magically scratch or bite at danger that might approach.

Thorns, nails, and needles are also a common feature of Ozark protective charm bags and rituals. The most common thorns used in the Ozarks, and the most powerful in my opinion, are from the honey locust tree (*Gleditsia triacanthos*). These thorns are easy to collect as the tree produces huge clusters on its bark, some more than a foot long on older trees. Another source for thorns is the common pear tree, an Ozark invasive in some places, which only produces thorns as a sapling and on the shoots that occasionally grow up around the base of the tree. On occasion, the prickles of the rosebush, blackberry cane, and greenbrier vine (*Smilax rotundifolia*) are used as well, although not technically considered thorns. Thorns by definition are modified branches of the plant or tree, whereas prickles appear on the actual "skin" or bark of the plant.

Nails and needles often serve the same purpose as thorns in being able to magically lame, or harm, evil before it gets close enough to hex you. In the old days, the deadliest nail you could use in any charm bag or ritual was one that was pulled directly from a coffin that was holding a dead body. These coffin nails were prized possessions of healers and magical practitioners and were used for everything from healing warts to killing demons. Along the same lines, needles that were used to sew burial shrouds were also prized magical items.

Today, some practitioners do still use these items in their work, although many have told me that they're definitely harder to acquire than they used to be. Most abide by another equally as powerful rule in certain spells: using new nails or needles. This is one that is much easier to find examples of today. The exact "newness" of these items is sometimes debated, however. Some say they have to be straight from an unopened package; others say that they just have to be unused and can come from out of a bigger container purchased from the store. The latter opinion is the more common one, I've found. Which makes sense, considering Ozarkers are known for their hatred of waste and I've yet to find a package in the store containing only one needle.

In addition to the buckeye and honey locust, other common protective plants include the sweetgum tree (*Liquidambar styraciflua*), Solomon's seal root (*Polygonatum* spp.), yarrow (*Achillea millefolium*), and the all-important red cedar (*Juniperus virginiana*). Some still consider red cedar, sassafras, and tobacco to be the "holy trinity" of Ozark plants. With these three plants, you can do anything medicinally or magically you need to do. Red cedar has long been a protecting plant in Ozark folk culture. Its leaves and berries are used in amulets for healing and protection, and its smoke is used to cleanse the home of evil energies. The simplest ward for protection can be made from red cedar leaves placed inside a small cloth bag that is then tied closed with three knots.

SEEKING HELP FROM THE OTHERWORLD

Protection has also traditionally come from petitioning spirits of the land, angelic guardians, or even family ghosts for aid. The land spirits, which include the powerful Little People, are often a favored choice today. In the old days this relationship was often hidden behind the use of "angels" or "angel guides" instead of saying the Little People or fairies, who were often associated with witchcraft. Today, though, many modern practitioners have helping spirits from amongst the Little People or other denizens of the wilderness. This is often seen as a difficult road, however, as the Little People often want certain things in return for their gifts. Ozark folklore features many tales about such exchanges, which often don't work in the requestor's favor.

Ancestral spirits are often easier to work with as protectors because they know and care for us. Of course, about this time I'm sure you're remembering some ancestors who you'd rather not have hanging around you all the time. No matter who you are or where you're from, we all have blemishes on our families and past. According to traditional Ozark spiritualism (as I've been taught, anyway), our ancestors who want to watch over and protect us will naturally step forward when the time is right and when we're ready to see them. Chances are they've always been there watching over us and we just didn't have the eyes to see them. These protectors aren't always from our family but might also be what I like to call *ancestors of the work*. These are particularly powerful for healers and witches as they can add their own power to our work. If you're worried about some of your less-than-friendly ancestors popping up in your work, all I have to say is trust that you also have much more powerful guides and protectors around you that want you to grow and succeed.

Seeking protection from the otherworld comes in a number of forms, but generally speaking it involves offering these spirits gifts in exchange for their services. Traditionally, gift giving for both the Little People and ancestors was mixed into certain holiday festivities, usually Christmas Eve. At this time, the spirits who watch over the home and family would be given their own plate of food and drink and also invited to join in the merriment. In some cases, depending upon the family's connection to the spirits, they might be served first, before anyone else, out of respect. As I was once told, you never want to have a party and not invite your house spirits to join in. This risks them getting offended and leaving, or worse, playing tricks on you.

This sort of devotion to the Little People and land spirits doesn't just fall on holidays for some people. Many Ozarkers have their own personal rituals for including certain spiritual forces in their daily lives, although few would actually ever admit to doing this. For instance, a farmer who keeps a solitary "fairy tree" or "witch tree" in the middle of their field for fear that cutting it down might offend the Little People. Or others who meticulously attend to natural springs near their homes lest neglecting one of these sacred sites might incur the wrath of the spirits who live there. One friend of mine told me about her aunt who would refresh a small bowl of milk set out on her mantelpiece everyday as an offering to her house brownies. My friend said that one day when she was a child her aunt let her pour the milk into the bowl, but she spilled a little. Her aunt went pale and shook her head, saying, "You better clean it up! The brownies won't like that at all."

RITUAL FOR PROTECTION WHILE TRAVELING USING THE BRIAR CHARM

MAGICAL TIMING: Full moon; waxing moon; Tuesday or Sunday; Aries or Leo

INGREDIENTS:

- Cloth bag with drawstring top, white
- Juniper or camphor essential oil
- 3 nails, new
- Paper square, white or blue, 5 inches by 5 inches
- Pen, blue
- Red cedar bark, dried (*Juniperus virginiana*) or juniper berries
- Salt
- String, white, 3 feet
- Tobacco leaves, dried (*Nicotiana tabacum* or *N. rustica*)

SPELL: In blue ink, write your full name three times horizontally in the center of a piece of new paper. The names should be one on top of the other like this:

FIRST MIDDLE LAST

FIRST MIDDLE LAST

FIRST MIDDLE LAST

Around the three names write this phrase clockwise in a circle: "A briar wall is a farmer's pain! Pain not me but my enemy. The briar is tall, the briar is wide. This briar has no gate but for my own feet. Prick and prickle, be swords, be spears!" It does not have to be a complete circle, and it can also spiral out if you run out of space. Just make sure you continue to write in a clockwise direction.

After this, fold the paper around some red cedar bark or juniper berries, a pinch of tobacco, a pinch of salt, and three new nails. After carefully folding up this packet, wrap it closed with your string and tie with three knots. Place this packet inside your white cloth bag, pull the top closed, and seal with another three knots. Anoint the bag with three drops of juniper or camphor essential oil.

Carry this charm with you while traveling, especially when you might be going to a new place and wish to be protected. Anoint again with juniper or camphor essential oils on the new and full moon to recharge.

VARIATIONS:

- If you don't have red cedar bark, you can also use juniper berries (*Juniperus communis*).

- The briar charm can also be used to protect the home from evil influences. In this ritual, you will repeat the phrase that appears in the spell section three times over three lengths of greenbrier (*Smilax rotundifolia*), then tie the bundle together with some white string and three knots. This protective charm can be hung outside the home above any entrance.

BIBLE VERSE: You can replace the verbal charm in the original spell with Psalm 3:3–6. "But you, O Lord, are a shield around me, my glory, and the one who lifts up my head. I cry aloud to the Lord, and he answers me from his holy hill. I lie down and sleep; I wake again, for the Lord sustains me. I am not afraid of ten thousands of people who have set themselves against me all around."

NOTES: This ritual makes use of a powerful image known to all Ozarkers, the dreaded greenbrier. Sometimes the word *briar* also refers to blackberry canes, but most often it is the greenbrier vine (*Smilax rotundifolia*), which grows fast and can twist itself into thorny, impassable walls in the forest called briar "breaks." It truly is the "farmer's pain," as stated in the verbal charm. But, in many Ozark rituals like this one, the image of the briar wall is invoked instead of cursed. It goes back to the laid-back philosophy of hillfolk to make the best out of any situation. For example, several Ozarkers I've met have lovingly referred to their soilless, stony yards as "rock farms." Or, as one healer told me, "If you step on a thorn, use the thorn," meaning that sometimes the best tools we can use for our magic are the ones nature gives to us.

RITUAL FOR A PROTECTIVE FENCE

MAGICAL TIMING: Waxing moon; Tuesday or Friday; Aries or Taurus

INGREDIENTS:

- Asafetida powder (*Ferula assa-foetida*)
- Camphor essential oil

- Gloves
- Knife
- 4 red cedar sticks (*Juniperus virginiana*), 1 foot long each
- Stockpot or bucket
- Tobacco leaves, dried (*Nicotiana tabacum* or *N. rustica*)
- Water

CAUTIONS: Do not drink this mixture. Camphor and tobacco can be fatal when consumed. Be sure to wear gloves when making this ritual mixture. The pungent odor of asafetida and camphor is difficult to wash off and can irritate the skin. I recommend performing this ritual outside to avoid stinking up your house.

SPELL: Start by finding your red cedar sticks. Each one should be around a foot long and have three prongs on one end. If you can't find these, two prongs will work, or none. Once gathered, soak the four sticks in a mixture of water, asafetida powder, camphor essential oil, and loose tobacco, all put into a pot or bucket large enough to hold the sticks underwater, or as best you can. I like to use a large stainless-steel stockpot that is easy to clean later on. Asafetida power can be purchased at most Indian grocery stores, called *hing* in Hindi. It can also be purchased online.

Recite this phrase over the sticks and water three times: "Once a great evil beast roamed the land from north to south, from east to west. None could save themselves from its wrath. A prayer went up to the sky and help came. Four birds came from the east and each bought with them a wand of white flame. Four stakes from north to south and east to west and slayed the beast."

Soak your sticks overnight, then dry them in the sun. Sharpen the ends opposite to the three prongs with a knife. Take and drive each stake into the earth on the north, south, east, and west sides of your house. Start with east, then proceed in a clockwise direction. You can repeat the verbal charm as you work, or carry with you an incense burner with smoking red cedar leaves.

VARIATIONS: The simplest form of this ritual is just using four red cedar stakes and driving them into the ground on the four sides of your home in a clockwise direction. While you don't need any more ingredients than that, the asafetida, camphor, and tobacco included in this recipe do make for a powerful magical fence.

BIBLE VERSE: You can replace the verbal charm in the original spell with Psalm 5:11–12. "But let all who take refuge in you rejoice; let them ever sing for joy. Spread your protection over them, so that those who love your name may exult in you. For you bless the righteous, O Lord; you cover them with favor as with a shield."

NOTES: The most powerful stakes for protective rituals like this one are said to be gathered from trees growing with their roots in running water. You often find red cedar trees like this growing along creeks and rivers.

A HOUSE CHARM BAG

MAGICAL TIMING: New moon to full moon; Friday; Taurus

INGREDIENTS:

- Camphor essential oil or gin
- Cloth bag with drawstring top, white
- 3 nails, new
- 3 needles for sewing, new
- Paper square, blue, 6 inches by 6 inches
- Pen, blue
- 12 red cedar berries, fresh or dried (*Juniperus virginiana*)
- Silver bowl or silver item
- String, blue, 3 feet
- 3 thorns, honey locust (*Gleditsia triacanthos*)

SPELL: Start on the new moon, preferably in Taurus. In this ritual, you will be blessing your charm bag daily until the full moon.

Once you have your ingredients gathered, write the SATOR AREPO square in the center of your square of blue paper in blue ink:

$$
\begin{array}{ccccc}
S & A & T & O & R \\
A & R & E & P & O \\
T & E & N & E & T \\
O & P & E & R & A \\
R & O & T & A & S
\end{array}
$$

After this, surround the square with these words written clockwise in the shape of a heart, also in blue ink: "This home is sealed, this home is protected. From all evils, from all sickness that roams the land. From all curses, from all hexes, from all unwanted guests. May this home prosper. May our cups never run dry. May our plates always be filled. A white flame at every door and window. A protector on every wall."

Next, fold the paper around twelve red cedar berries, then wrap with your string and tie closed with three knots. Once you've done this, put the paper into your white cloth bag. Add the three new nails, three thorns, and three new needles. Finish by tying the bag closed with three knots. Anoint with three drops of camphor essential oil or gin. Place your bag in a silver bowl, or you can use a regular bowl and add in a silver item like a ring, chain, coin, etc., making sure it is touching the bag at all times. Anoint the bag with three drops of camphor essential oil or gin every day along with the verbal charm until the full moon.

On the day of the full moon, anoint the bag one more time with three drops of your camphor oil or gin, then hang on the inside of your house near or above any door leading outside. I usually make two at a time for clients so that they can hang one above their front door and one above their back door. You can always make more depending on how many doors you have in your house that lead outside.

Anoint again with three drops of camphor essential oil or gin on the new and full moon to recharge.

VARIATIONS:

- Instead of red cedar berries, you can also use common juniper berries (*Juniperus communis*) if they are easier to find.

- You can also use alternatives to the honey locust thorns, including pear tree thorns, as mentioned in this chapter's introduction, or even the prickles off a rosebush, blackberry cane, or greenbrier vine. You can also use wooden toothpicks if no thorns are available.

- Solomon's seal root (*Polygonatum* spp.) or sweetgum bark (*Liquidambar styraciflua*) are both amazing additional plants that you can add to this charm bag for added benefit.

BIBLE VERSE: You can replace the verbal charm in the original spell with Psalm 11. "In the Lord I take refuge; how can you say to me, 'Flee like a bird to the mountains; for look, the wicked bend the bow, they have fitted their arrow to the string, to shoot in the dark at the upright in heart. If the foundations are destroyed, what can the righteous do?' The Lord is in his holy temple; the Lord's throne is in heaven. His eyes behold, his gaze examines humankind. The Lord tests the righteous and the wicked, and his soul hates the lover of violence. On the wicked he will rain coals of fire and sulfur; a scorching wind shall be the portion of their cup. For the Lord is righteous; he loves righteous deeds; the upright shall behold his face."

NOTES: This amulet makes use of the famous SATOR AREPO magic square that has ancient roots. It likely came into the Ozarks by way of Pennsylvania German immigrants and their *Powwowing* or *Braucherei* folk magic traditions, specifically those derived from John George Hohman's famous book of magic, *The Long-Lost Friend*. Ozarkers have taken a much more simplified view of what has been a complicated area of folk magic. I've seen several magic squares in use around the area, but the SATOR AREPO square is by far the most popular. Magicians and practitioners have developed the complicated methods for figuring the letters and numbers contained within the squares since the Middle Ages. Amongst Ozarkers, these squares have been passed down or picked up from books and never formulated from scratch. I've yet to meet a modern Ozark practitioner who could fully explain the significance of the magic square to me, and I myself don't fully understand the nuanced magical formulas used in the process. Like many of my informants, I hold to the view that if it works, it works, whether I understand it or not.

House charm bags like this one have been found throughout the Ozarks. Often they were put inside of walls when the house was being built or hidden away for safe keeping in the attic. This form of folk magic would have no doubt raised a few suspicious eyebrows from the more conservative types in the old Ozarks, so while they were very important to many, charm bags were commonly kept secret, oftentimes even from many of the people living in the house. One old man I met was shocked to find a charm bag hidden away in the wall of his family's cabin he was renovating. It bore a faded—but still visible—embroidered design of the family surname on the outside of the bag. The man guessed it was his mother who had made it, but he was shocked because she was a staunch churchgoer her entire life and often sternly commented on the "witchish ways" of others in their community.

A PROTECTING HEART AMULET

MAGICAL TIMING: Full moon; Tuesday or Friday; Taurus or Scorpio

INGREDIENTS:

- Cloth, red
- Embroidery thread, blue, enough to sew the heart

SPELL: Take and cut out a small heart from your red cloth. With your blue embroidery thread, sew the initials of the one you wish to protect on the two lobes of the heart, with the first and middle initial being on the left and the last name initial on the right. Then sew the date you are creating the amulet on the bottom of the heart.

You can then stitch this amulet inside your loved one's shirt or coat to protect them from all harm. Sewing this near the heart of the garment is best.

VARIATIONS: This simple amulet can be added to in a number of ways. You can, for example, cut out two hearts and then sew them together to make a little parcel. These are usually filled with protective plants like red cedar (*Juniperus virginiana*) or yarrow (*Achillea millefolium*) and then sewn into the inside of a coat or shirt. I even saw one example where a more modern witch included a small square of paper with the famous SATOR AREPO square written on it that was added behind the heart before it was sewn into her son's coveralls.

BIBLE VERSE: You can repeat Psalm 36:11–12 while you sew. You can also even write or sew it directly onto the heart itself. "Do not let the foot of the arrogant tread on me, or the hand of the wicked drive me away. There the evildoers lie prostrate; they are thrust down, unable to rise."

NOTES:

- I've seen a few of these amulets "out in the wild," as it were, while collecting stories and remedies. They aren't just a gesture of affection; the people I've met who wore hearts like these all swore by their effectiveness in warding off harm. One old man I met still wore his even though he was retired from his dangerous job at a cattle auction. His wife made him one of these hearts and stitched it into his overalls after he came home one day with an almost-broken knee from being kicked by a bull. After that, the old man swore every time a cow would go to kick him they'd "miss by a mile," as he said.

- There's a long tradition in the Ozarks of sewing charm bags and other items into clothing, so the use of this particular amulet isn't surprising. One informant did tell me she'd heard it was a common practice during the Civil War, when women would sew hearts into their loved one's uniforms as a form of protection. I haven't been able to verify this anecdote.

MAKING A PROTECTIVE LADDER OF STRING

MAGICAL TIMING: Waxing moon; full moon; Friday; Taurus

INGREDIENTS:

- 1 hole stone
- 7 honey locust thorns (*Gleditsia triacanthos*) or new nails
- String, white, 4 feet

SPELL: Take a length of string about four feet long. Form a knot at the left end of the string, but don't close it completely. Blow through the knot and then recite this verbal charm: "Evil be tripped, be caught, be snared! Evil be bashed and beaten! Step on thorns, all evil that would enter this home!" As you finish the charm, close the knot around a honey locust thorn or new nail. An additional knot might need to be tied to hold the thorn in place.

Repeat the blowing, verbal charm, and knot tying for all seven of your thorns. Finish by tying your hole stone, also called a hag stone, to the bottom of the string and then hang your ladder outside any entrance into your house.

You can smoke your ladder with red cedar (*Juniperus virginiana*) on the new and full moon to recharge.

VARIATIONS: You don't have to just use thorns or nails in your ladder, although these items are the most common found in the Ozarks. You can also use leaves and branches from protective plants, sticks of red cedar or yarrow stalks for instance. The most important aspects of the ritual are the sacred numbers (seven in this case), blowing/praying through the knots, and the general shape of the ladder. Everything else can be changed around to suit your practice. The hole stone at the bottom does have significance in the context of the ritual, as I mention in the notes. If you don't have one, though, you can replicate the meaning by tying a loop of string at the bottom.

BIBLE VERSE: You can replace the verbal charm in the original spell with Job 1:10. "Have you not put a fence around him and his house and all that he has, on every side? You have blessed the work of his hands, and his possessions have increased in the land."

NOTES: These objects are also traditionally called *witch ladders*, and predate any modern popularity surrounding the warding object. I've seen them made with thorns, nails, and even sharpened red cedar twigs. Today, many recipes for witch ladders use feathers, but I haven't seen this form in the Ozarks. The legend behind the protective ladder is an interesting one. I've only ever heard this explanation from one Ozark informant, but she was a wise woman and healer so I trust she was honest in her story. According to her, in order for evil to enter into your home, it has to climb down each rung of the ladder and the thorns stick them each time, making them weaker and weaker. If they do manage to get all the way down, they'll fall into the hole in the hag stone and get trapped "like in a whirlpool," as she said.

RITUAL TO PROTECT YOURSELF FROM BEING DECEIVED

MAGICAL TIMING: Full moon; Wednesday; Gemini or Pisces

INGREDIENTS:

- Heat-safe bowl/plate
- Incense charcoal and burner, with metal tongs
- Lighter or matches
- 12 paper squares, blue, 2 inches by 2 inches
- Sweetgum resin or dried bark (*Liquidambar styraciflua*)
- Yarrow flowers, dried (*Achillea millefolium*)

SPELL: Begin by preparing the incense that you will be burning during the ritual. This consists of equal parts sweetgum sap or bark and yarrow flowers. If you can, let the sweetgum sap dry out completely before using. If you use it fresh, you won't be able to powder it, but you can grind up the yarrow flowers finely and then mix it with the fresh sap to form incense balls. You can also use frankincense resin if sweetgum is difficult to acquire.

Once your incense is ready, take your twelve paper squares and draw a single eye on each one. The corners of the eyes should all match with the corners of the paper, like this:

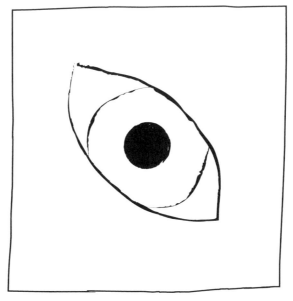

Then go outside, preferably to a flat, concrete area like a porch. You can also do this ritual in the grass, just make sure it is a level spot. Bring your paper squares, an incense burner with charcoal, metal tongs, matches or lighter, and a dish for burning. This dish can be made of any material, as long as it is heatproof and won't itself burn. I like to use either an old metal stockpot or a large clay dish like you can buy for underneath potted plants.

When you've found your spot, sit down and place your burning dish in front of you on the left and the incense burner on the right. Next, take your twelve eye papers and place them in a square around you in a clockwise direction, beginning with the upper leftmost corner. Your shape should look like this:

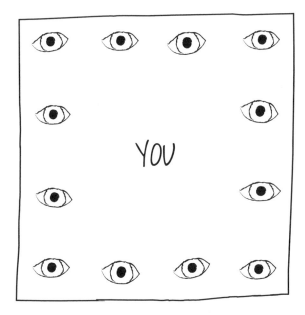

After all the papers have been placed, repeat this verbal charm: "What has been unseen, I now see. My eyes are opened to the truth I have not known. Let every veil placed over my eyes be burned in this fire."

Light your charcoal by holding it in a lighter flame using the metal tongs. Once the charcoal is hot, add some of your incense mixture to the charcoal and let it smoke. Starting again with the upper leftmost corner of the eye papers, take each square and waft it through the incense smoke and then burn it in the pot or on the clay dish. Do this in a counterclockwise direction this time, until all twelve of the papers have been burned. Once cooled, take the ashes of the papers and bury them in the roots of a sweetgum tree, throw them into a moving body of water, or flush them down the toilet.

VARIATIONS: In cases where you think you are perhaps being deceived by a specific individual and would like to magically break through this, you can write their full name on the back of each of the eye squares. You can also attach some identifying materials to the paper using a drop of beeswax, if you so choose. If you are targeting a specific individual, alter the verbal charm in the spell section to go like this: "What has been unseen, I now see. My eyes are opened to the truth I have not known. Let every veil placed over my eyes by (FIRST MIDDLE LAST) be burned in this fire."

If you don't know the name, you can also replace this with "MY ENEMY," both written on the eye squares and inserted into the verbal charm.

BIBLE VERSE: You can replace the verbal charm in the original spell with Psalm 10. "Why, O Lord, do you stand far off? Why do you hide yourself in times of trouble? In arrogance the wicked persecute the poor—let them be caught in the schemes they have devised. For the wicked boast of the desires of their heart, those greedy for gain curse and renounce the Lord. In the pride of their countenance the wicked say, 'God will not seek it out'; all their thoughts are, 'There is no God.' Their ways prosper at all times; your judgments are on high, out of their sight; as for their foes, they scoff at them. They think in their heart, 'We shall not be moved; throughout all generations we shall not meet adversity.' Their mouths are filled with cursing and deceit and oppression; under their tongues are mischief and iniquity. They sit in ambush in the villages; in hiding places they murder the innocent. Their eyes stealthily watch for the helpless; they lurk in secret like a lion in its covert; they lurk that they may seize the poor; they seize the poor and drag them off in their net. They stoop, they crouch, and the helpless fall by their might. They think in their heart, 'God has forgotten, he has hidden his face, he will never see it.' Rise up, O Lord; O God, lift up your hand; do not forget the oppressed. Why do the wicked renounce God, and say in their hearts, 'You will not call us to account'? But you do see! Indeed you note trouble and grief, that you may take it into your hands; the helpless commit themselves to you; you have been the helper of the orphan. Break the arm of the wicked and evildoers; seek out their wickedness until you find none. The Lord is king forever and ever; the nations shall perish from his land. O Lord, you will hear the desire of the meek; you will strengthen their heart, you will incline your ear to do justice for the orphan and the oppressed, so that those from earth may strike terror no more."

NOTES: The practitioner who gave me this spell worked it into her monthly full moon routine along with traditional cleanses. She said performing this ritual every full moon helped keep her "spiritual eyes open" throughout the month.

RITUAL TO PROTECT YOUR HOME USING AN OIL LAMP

MAGICAL TIMING: Full moon; Friday; Taurus

INGREDIENTS:

- Matches or a lighter
- Oil lamp with paraffin lamp oil
- Paper, blue
- Red cedar berries, fresh or dried (*Juniperus virginiana*)

CAUTIONS: Paraffin oil does give off smoke when burned that can irritate the eyes and lungs. I recommend burning your lamp in a room where you can open a window for ventilation. I don't recommend leaving your lamp burning overnight. There are odorless and smokeless varieties of lamp oil that you can purchase.

SPELL: The most basic way of using an oil lamp for your magic rituals is to simply write your prayer, name, or petition on a small strip of white paper and then drop it into the reservoir of your oil lamp. Lighting the lamp will then activate your petition.

But, for a more involved ritual, I suggest using blue paper and red cedar berries to connect to the power of protection magic through symbolic color and ingredients. Once added to the lamp's reservoir, light the wick on the full moon and/or on Friday for added magical benefit. The protecting light of the lamp, fueled by the magical ingredients and specific petition you added, will flow through your home.

You can set up your lamp in a more elaborate ritual space, if you'd like. For protection work, I recommend surrounding the lamp with three greenbrier (*Smilax rotundifolia*) vines twisted together into the shape of a circle. Leave this magic "fence" up whenever you're doing protection work. When you do light your lamp, you can repeat this verbal charm: "As this light dispels the darkness, so let all sickness, curses, evil eyes, and danger be dispelled from around and inside my home." Burn your lamp and visualize a wall of blue fire encircling the outside of your home. The fire is cool to the touch, but burns away all sickness and curses that might try to pass through it. Only those things that are meant for your healing and blessing are allowed through. Sit with this visualization as long as you would like.

VARIATIONS: If you don't have an oil lamp, you can still perform this ritual using a candle. In this case, find a blue candle; any size will work. Write out your prayers and petitions on a piece of blue paper, then place it on a flat table with your blue candle standing on top in a suitable holder. Or, if you're using a jar candle, you can just place it directly on the paper. You can also include a greenbrier ring like the one used in the original ritual. Light your candle and repeat the visualization recommended in the spell section.

BIBLE VERSE: You can replace the verbal charm in the original spell with John 1:1–5. "In the beginning was the Word, and the Word was with God, and the Word was God. He was in the beginning with God. All things came into being through him, and without him not one thing came into being. What has come into being in him was life, and the life was the light of all people. The light shines in the darkness, and the darkness did not overcome it."

NOTES: In the old days, before electricity became more widely available, oil lamps were a common feature in nearly every Ozark home. Now, many people still have these lamps that they've inherited from family or found at a garage sale or flea market. While they aren't important to our survival anymore, the oil lamp has represented so much to hillfolk throughout the years. It is literally the embodiment of light, which connects symbolically to the hearth, home, family, warmth, love, and survival. The light from the lamp dispels the darkness around us and gives clarity to our vision. It's no wonder that fire in general—and the oil lamp specifically—has been used for magic and healing since our ancient ancestors first discovered that a spark, when held up to tinder, will ignite. The oil lamp is such a powerful feature of Ozark folk culture as well as our healing traditions. I recommend that anyone branching off in the direction of Ozark folk magic have one in their home.

RETRIBUTION

PLANET: Mars, Saturn

ZODIAC: Aries, Scorpio

DAY: Tuesday

COLOR: Black

ITEMS:

- Nails / needles / thorns
- Spite doll
- Witch balls (witch bullets)

PLANTS:

- Black nightshade (*Solanum americanum*)
- Bull nettle (*Solanum carolinense*)
- Honey locust (*Gleditsia triacanthos*)
- Jimsonweed (*Datura stramonium*)
- Mayapple (*Podophyllum peltatum*)
- Pokeweed (*Phytolacca americana*)

Retribution work has always been a complicated subject in the Ozarks, even today. Let me first explain exactly what I mean when I say *retribution work*. This includes all rites and rituals for returning hexes back to their sender and working to diminish the power of your enemy. This isn't just curse work but is situated within the traditional framework of Ozark magical ethics. First and foremost, I don't at all advocate for the *curse-anyone-you-want-for-any-reason* approach to magic. At the same time, I don't adhere to the *curses-are-dangerous-and-will-always-backfire* approach either. And to be honest, neither path really represents folk magic in the Ozarks or what I've seen from other folk magic traditions in the least bit. I've mentioned this many times, but one of the most important foundational pieces to Ozark folk magic and healing is understanding the inherent neutrality of magic. Ozark workers, for the most part, have then worked in this gray area. Swinging to either extreme would be seen as a detriment to the Ozark practitioner's work.

WORKING WITH BOTH HANDS

The story wasn't much different in the old Ozarks either. Many people have a vision of "traditional" folk magic practices as being something much more rooted in religious piety and rural conservatism. To some extent this is true, but only on the surface level. Practitioners in the old Ozarks did work more with the Bible, angels, and other religious symbols, and yes, they did fit themselves into the conservative culture around them. We have to remember, though, that this was for survival. I've met many healers across the mountains who exemplify what I'm talking about here. One praying granny I met was a pillar of the local church community and had been for most of her life. She told me one time that if she had never had kids, she would have been a preacher or missionary. She used her Bible and traditional prayers alone in all the work she did. When we spoke in larger groups, she always talked about the demonic power of witchcraft and how it could take hold of a healer quickly. When we spoke just the two of us, she loved telling me about all the Bible verses she knew for cursing her enemies.

Healers and magical practitioners in the Ozarks have always done everything they could to not stand out, despite their gift and profession. In the old days—and to some extent, this is still true in certain areas—standing out because of your magical abilities meant constantly being under scrutiny from the community. This is one reason so many older healers were also local preachers or, at the very least, highly pious. While some might have used this as a way of moving the eye of the community away from their work, others saw a vital link between their power and their piety. On some level, though, all practitioners knew that standing out was a sure way to be labeled as a witch and tried to avoid this at all costs.

One certain way to make a healer stand out was practicing anything akin to witch-craft. According to the traditional Ozark division of practitioners and magic, on one end of the spectrum you have the healer who heals and always uses their power for good. On the opposite end from the healer is the figure of the witch, who always uses their power to hurt, kill, or maim people, or to steal from the community at large. While both of these sides of the spectrum might have used the same exact magic in very similar ways, only the "fruits of their labor" and whether those were for "good" or "evil" would determine their status in the community. The healer then did everything they could to remain on their side of the divide, and the witch did everything they could to go unnoticed by the community while being free to kill and steal to their heart's content.

As it turns out, the story is far more complicated than this. Even in the so-called "traditional times" of Ozark magic, healers didn't just heal. Healers also threw hexes back at their senders. They crushed the power of rival healers in order to vie for clients. They cursed farms, crops, and livestock of clients who failed to pay them. They also, at times, pointed the finger at local "witches" to take the heat off of their own work. Ozark practitioners have always worked in this gray area of magic, even when they had to hide behind more pious masks. In many cases, some healers openly justified their work as being more pious than that of others because, as one healer told me, she worked "like God himself works... he gives with one hand and takes with the other."

Context is always vitally important, especially when we see magical work that goes against our preconceived notions of what might be "traditional" or not. Retribution work is as Ozark as any other. If you are a practitioner who isn't comfortable adding any of these spells to your own practice, they can easily be left out. I do want to reiterate that these rituals are based in the "return to sender" philosophy of hillfolk magic. These spells are reactionary, not outright aggressive. In all cases represented here, the other party has first worked against you in some way.

MATERIA MALEFICUM

Unlike many of the other spell sections, the items and plants for working retribution are also ingredients that would be associated with traditional witchcraft. These include items like spite dolls, nails, thorns, and certain poisonous plants predominantly from the night-shade family (*Solanaceae*). Ozark spite dolls are quite famous in the area and come from a long line of similar variations stretching all the way back to multiple folk traditions across

Europe. Using a doll as a representative for a patient or victim is by no means limited to European folk traditions and seems to be a world phenomenon. In the Ozarks, spite dolls are usually made from corn husks, paper, or even beeswax. They are used in both healing and cursing rituals as a way of working on a person remotely. This magical connection is created by inserting or attaching certain identifying materials like hair, fingernail clippings, clothing, or even a name to the doll. Some Ozarkers I've met have referred to these objects as "Voodoo dolls" mostly because of the influence of media, in particular horror movies. *Spite doll* seems to be a traditional term that predates any contact from Hollywood.

In addition to protection work, nails and thorns have also traditionally been used in retribution spells and rituals. In this case, the deadliest nails would be those taken directly from a coffin, which were seen as having been imbued with magical energy, specifically related to death and cursing. Honey locust thorns are another Ozark favorite to use. These are sometimes stabbed into spite dolls to hurt the targeted individual or, in many cases, are used as "darts" that are magically thrown at someone by way of a specific ritual. These objects themselves are almost never used just as they are, meaning healers and practitioners choose to work through magical symbolism rather than actually stabbing people with nails and thorns. The same applies to poisons, which are applied through magical means as a way of affecting the targeted individual. In the ancient past, however, the story was often very different as the magical power of certain curses was often heightened by the poisonous nature of their ingredients.

Another magical item once considered deadly by Ozark hillfolk was the dreaded witch ball or witch bullet, as it's sometimes called. These were small balls made from beeswax and various other resins, plants, and magical ingredients that were "shot" or thrown at a victim in order to deliver a quick hex. In most cases, the victim would either become seriously ill from this contact or die on the spot. Witch balls aren't something I teach how to make, but they are an interesting tidbit from Ozark folk culture that have provided many riveting fireside tales.

Poisonous plants have long been associated with witchcraft and hex magic. This lineage of folk belief stretches back to ancient Europe, especially with species from the nightshade family. Favored poisonous plants of the Ozarks include three nightshade species: black nightshade, bull nettle (*Solanum carolinense*), and jimsonweed, as well as two other non-nightshade plants, mayapple and pokeweed. All of these plants have also been used in traditional Ozark herbalism to help with a variety of ailments. For magical practitioners, though, these species in particular were favored because of their more sinister properties. Application of these poisons varied from ritual to ritual, but in many cases, I've seen spite dolls stuffed with one or more of these plant species, or smoked with their burning roots and foliage, as a part of the retribution formula. In some cases, part of the spite doll itself is sometimes formed from dried branches of these plants, in particular black nightshade and jimsonweed. Other times, the simple presence of the plant in the ritual—either physically or through invoking the plant in verbal charms and prayers—is more than sufficient to gain some added magical help in the work.

Traditionally, after any curse or retribution work, an Ozark practitioner or healer took a quick cleansing bath to remove any of the work that might have remained on their own body. It was believed that traces of the poisons or cursing words that were used could stick to and defile their own body if they weren't careful. This impurity could then affect their work in other areas like healing and blessing. Chapter 4's "Ritual to Cleanse Using a Bath" is a great way to finish any of the retribution rituals in this chapter.

WORKING DYNAMICALLY AND DIFFERENTLY

As with all other aspects of Ozark folk magic, retribution rituals vary significantly from practitioner to practitioner. Many witches today have been influenced by practices from outside the range of Ozark traditional magic, bringing in rites and spells from across the witching world. The spells I've collected for this chapter are all of the more traditional Ozark variety, but they can easily be incorporated into any practice.

In my workshops and lectures on the subject, I've often been asked about spells and rituals that use more "left-handed" items, or ingredients associated with more malign magics. In the Ozarks, these often include things like poisonous plants, animal bones, blood, or organs, as well as ingredients from graveyards like dirt or moss. In many cases, these items were dreamed up by nonpractitioners to add a spooky edge to their fireside stories. In some cases, though, yes, Ozark practitioners have used these ingredients in a variety of practices. People are sometimes worried about not being an effective witch because they can't stomach working with some of these items. To that I say, it's all right! At least with Ozark folk magic, you can easily replace most items in a ritual with anything you have on hand. Take, for instance, an old-time ritual for retribution against a criminal. You're supposed to take a goat or pig heart, stab it with three coffin nails while reciting the criminal's name, then hang it up in your chimney so that the fire eventually burns it away completely. This is a fascinating and powerful ritual that can be accomplished just as well using an apple or potato as the container and honey locust thorns for the nails. Easy!

Replacement items like these are just as "traditional," so don't think you are somehow missing out just because you aren't comfortable working with things like blood, bones, or organs. Even the poisonous plants I've listed in these spells can be substituted with any Mars- or Saturn-aligned species you have on hand or have available at your local witchy supply store. For me and many other Ozark practitioners, your intention is key to any spell! At the end of the day, the mind, will, and imagination are the most powerful tools we have.

RITUAL AGAINST YOUR ENEMY OR HEXER

MAGICAL TIMING: Waning moon; Tuesday; Scorpio

INGREDIENTS:

- Charcoal briquettes
- Jimsonweed leaves and/or flowers, dried (*Datura stramonium*)
- Lighter or matches
- Paper square, red, 5 inches by 5 inches
- Pen, red
- Identifying materials (optional)

CAUTIONS: All parts of jimsonweed (*Datura stramonium*), but especially the seeds, can be deadly when ingested. I recommend wearing gloves when handling the fresh leaves and flowers as they can sometimes cause contact dermatitis. Do not inhale the smoke from jimsonweed, as it can cause lung irritation and make you dizzy.

SPELL: Begin this ritual by gathering identifying materials from your target. If you don't have any of these, you can also write the full name of your enemy three times in the center of the paper square in red ink, one on top of the other, like this:

FIRST MIDDLE LAST

FIRST MIDDLE LAST

FIRST MIDDLE LAST

If you don't know the name of your enemy or you aren't able to identify the one who sent the curse, you can also write "MY ENEMY" or "CURSE SENDER" instead.

After this, write these words clockwise in a circle or square around the names: "Body burn, from head to toe. Body ache, from arm to arm, leg to leg. Burn and ache until you stop. Burn and ache until your work stops. Jimsonweed's roots grow deep, into rock, into stone, into flesh. Jimsonweed take root and deliver my message quick."

After writing these words, fold the paper around your identifying materials and some jimsonweed leaves and flowers; these can be fresh or dried. Next, while outside, light your charcoal in a heat-safe grill or firepit. Your charcoal briquettes may or may not already have lighter fluid in them. If not, you might need to add some to get the coals started. Once hot, throw the paper onto the coals while reciting the same charm from earlier three times.

Let the coals burn to ash completely. Once they are cooled, gather some up and blow them in the direction of your enemy's house or dust the ground where they might walk. If you don't know their identity, you can also blow some of the ash in the seven directions, clockwise, beginning facing the west. These directions are west, north, east, south, back to west, then up, down, and center.

VARIATIONS: The most common variation of this ritual involves making a spite doll. Usually, it would be cut from paper so that you can also write the name of your enemy and the charm mentioned in the original ritual on the doll. You could also use cornhusks or wax and attach a piece of paper with this written information as well as any identifying materials before burning. If you have access to a photo of your hexer, this would be considered a higher-level identifying material. In that case, you would just write the verbal charm directly on the back of the photo.

BIBLE VERSE: You can replace the verbal charm in the original spell with Psalm 109:17–19. "He loved to curse; let curses come on him. He did not like blessing; may it be far from him. He clothed himself with cursing as his coat, may it soak into his body like water, like oil into his bones. May it be like a garment that he wraps around himself, like a belt that he wears every day."

NOTES: Jimsonweed is known in part for its long roots that can grow a lot deeper into the ground than one might expect. This is one reason farmers hate the plant. That and the fact that the poisonous seeds from the plant can get mixed up with grain, beans, or corn during harvesttime, thereby completely ruining the entire crop. Because of its long roots, the words in this ritual invoke jimsonweed to magically root itself into the target, causing all sorts of body aches and pains as a form of righteous vengeance. One countercharm I've heard for such "rooting" rites is to wash in rabbit or gopher droppings while invoking the power of the creature to come in and dig up the roots that were planted inside your body.

When I was given this spell originally, my informant used another of jimsonweed's names, Jamestown weed. It received this name because, according to legend, soldiers who were sent to quell Bacon's Rebellion ate some of the seeds and fell into a comedic stupor for several days.

RITUAL TO BIND YOUR ENEMY

MAGICAL TIMING: Waning moon; Tuesday; Aries or Scorpio

INGREDIENTS:

- Beeswax, melted
- Charcoal briquettes
- Cloth, black
- Matches or a lighter
- Paper square, red, 5 inches by 5 inches
- Pen or pencil
- 1 stalk of black nightshade (*Solanum americanum*) or jimsonweed (*Datura stramonium*)
- String, black, 5 feet
- String, black, 7 feet
- Identifying materials (optional)

CAUTIONS: Do not inhale the smoke from black nightshade (*Solanum americanum*) or jimsonweed (*Datura stramonium*), as both can irritate the lungs and throat. Work only outside, and try not to get too close to the smoke. Wear gloves when handling these plants as both can cause contact dermatitis. Do not ingest either plant.

SPELL: First, find a black nightshade or jimsonweed plant of good size and that is branching in at least two directions. Cut the plant so that the main stalk is intact along with the two branches, forming a Y shape. Strip off any leaves, berries, and additional branches and save them by setting them to the side.

Next, in the center of your paper square, write your enemy's name (or "MY ENEMY" if you don't know the name) three times horizontally in black ink, like this:

FIRST MIDDLE LAST

FIRST MIDDLE LAST

FIRST MIDDLE LAST

After this, rotate the page to the left (counterclockwise) a quarter turn. The names should now be standing vertically. Write this phrase three times horizontally across the names: "Be bound, be tied," just like you did with the names originally. Your paper should now look like this:

If you have any identifying materials from your enemy, now is the time to add them to your paper roll. Seal the materials in place with some melted beeswax. Then, roll the paper square around the tip of the main stem or "head" of the nightshade Y and seal there with a good amount of melted beeswax so that it won't fall off or move down the stalk. Let the beeswax dry.

Next, take your spite doll outside along with a piece of black string seven feet long and a piece five feet long. Light your charcoal. Your charcoal briquettes may or may not already have lighter fluid in them. If not, you might need to add some to get the coals started. While they heat up, wrap the seven-foot string counterclockwise around the two branches of the nightshade Y. Make sure to wrap tightly. These are the "legs" of your enemy. Repeat this phrase while wrapping: "(NAME or MY ENEMY), be bound, be tied! As strong as iron! As strong as the roots of the mountains are chained into the earth!"

Continue repeating the verbal charm until all the string is used, then tie three tight knots to seal the work. Take the berries and leaves you stripped from the plant earlier on and cast them onto the hot charcoal. Hold your spite doll in the smoke, but take care to wear a mask covering your face, as the fumes can make you light-headed. Repeat the verbal charm three more times. After smoking, wrap the spite doll in black cloth and tie closed with your five-foot black string. Keep it in a secret location. It is believed that as long as the spite doll is still bound, your enemy won't be able to work against you. This spell will last indefinitely until your enemy is able to recover the doll, uses their own magical methods to sever the connection, or destroys the power of the identifying materials you used.

VARIATIONS: Stalks of the mayapple plant (*Podophyllum peltatum*) are sometimes used in this ritual because they naturally form a Y shape when growing out of the ground. Care is taken to include the bulbous root of the plant, often called American mandrake, to represent the enemy's head as a part of the spite doll.

You can perform this ritual using a spite doll made from other materials as well. While using the nightshade and jimsonweed plant help add some extra power, you can also make a spite doll using paper or cornhusks and then smoke it with these plants as instructed in the original ritual.

BIBLE VERSE: You can replace the verbal charm in the original spell with Psalm 149:5–9. "Let the faithful exult in glory; let them sing for joy on their couches. Let the high praises of God be in their throats and two-edged swords in their hands, to execute vengeance on the nations and punishment on the peoples, to bind their kings with fetters and their nobles with chains of iron, to execute on them the judgment decreed. This is glory for all his faithful ones."

NOTES: Binding rituals like this one are used for a variety of purposes but mainly to prevent someone from working, or continuing their work, against you. In similar rituals performed for the public, binding might be aimed at preventing an abusive ex from coming onto a person's property or stopping someone's advancement in a career or even political office.

RITUAL TO PUT YOUR ENEMY UNDER A WATERFALL

MAGICAL TIMING: Waning moon; Tuesday; Scorpio

INGREDIENTS:

- Cloth, black
- 2 honey locust thorns
- Paper, white or red
- Pen, red
- 9 rocks, small
- String, black, 3 feet
- Beeswax, melted (optional)
- Identifying materials (optional)

CAUTIONS: Honey locust thorns are extremely sharp, so please take caution when handling these items. Especially be careful when harvesting them in the wild; this is how I myself have received the bulk of my thorn wounds.

SPELL: You're going to start this ritual by making your spite doll. Cut a human shape from a piece of paper. Make it fairly large so that it will be easy to work with. Write the name of your enemy (or the words "MY ENEMY") three times in the "heart" of the doll like this:

FIRST MIDDLE LAST

FIRST MIDDLE LAST

FIRST MIDDLE LAST

If you have any identifying materials from your enemy, seal them in place over the names with some beeswax and let it dry. Next, fold the two hands of the spite doll together and pierce with one of the honey locust thorns while saying, "(NAME or MY ENEMY), your hands are bound tight." Make sure to leave the thorn holding the hands closed. Fold the two feet together and pierce with the second thorn and say, "(NAME or MY ENEMY), your feet are bound tighter."

With the spite doll's hands and feet now held together with the honey locust thorns, place the doll onto the piece of black cloth. Lay nine small rocks on top of your doll while repeating this verbal charm for each rock: "A stone to weigh you down. A stone to hold you fast."

Once all nine of the rocks are on your spite doll, wrap all of this up in your cloth and tie closed with the black string, making sure neither the doll nor the rocks can fall out. Take this bundle out to a waterfall and place the bundle so that the water is constantly falling on it. Repeat this final verbal charm: "Water crash on your head! Water break your bones and your magic!"

Traditionally, most Ozark workers would leave items like these behind, where they were placed, but you can also take it home with you and repeat the waterfall placing and verbal charm whenever you sense that your enemy might be turning back against you. Let the closed bag and its contents dry out between placing rituals.

VARIATIONS:

- A couple workers I met also suggested doing this ritual with water from a gutter drain on your roof. Whenever it rains, place the bag so that water from the roof will constantly fall onto it. Use the same verbal charm that appears in the spell section.

- You can also bury your enemy in a lake, pond, or swamp by throwing your bundle full of rocks into the water and letting it sink to the bottom. I don't prefer this method as you will be leaving waste behind in a natural setting.

BIBLE VERSE: You can also recite Exodus 15:6–10 during all parts of the ritual. "Your right hand, O Lord, glorious in power—your right hand, O Lord, shattered the enemy. In the greatness of your majesty you overthrew your adversaries; you sent out your fury, it consumed them like stubble. At the blast of your nostrils the waters piled up, the floods stood up in a heap; the deeps congealed in the heart of the sea. The enemy said, 'I will pursue, I will overtake, I will divide the spoil, my desire shall have its fill of them. I will draw my sword, my hand shall destroy them.' You blew with your wind, the sea covered them; they sank like lead in the mighty waters."

NOTES: A similar ritual was recorded by Vance Randolph in *Ozark Magic and Folklore*. In this case, the practitioners would hang locks of a person's hair or their photograph under the eaves of their house when it was raining so that the water would pour over one of these items, thereby causing their target harm. Randolph also mentions that in some cases, the so-called witch would name an animal part (like teeth, bones, eyes, or even testicles) to be the corresponding body part on their target. Then the witch would leave the animal part under a waterfall to cause their enemy crippling pains.[3]

RITUAL TO ROT AWAY YOUR ENEMY USING AN APPLE

MAGICAL TIMING: Full moon; midnight; Tuesday; Aries

INGREDIENTS:

- Apple corer or metal poker
- Apple, whole
- Bull nettle leaves and/or chopped berries, dried (*Solanum carolinense*)
- Charcoal briquettes
- Knife
- Lighter or matches
- Paper square, red, 5 inches by 5 inches
- Pen, red
- Identifying materials (optional)

CAUTIONS: This ritual involves smoke from the bull nettle plant (*Solanum carolinense*), which is considered toxic. Take caution as the smoke can cause lung irritation and headaches if inhaled. Work only outside, and try not to get too close to the smoke. Take care when handling the plant as it has thorns and the fresh foliage is known to cause contact dermatitis. Do not ingest.

---

3. Randolph, *Ozark Magic and Folklore*, 279.

SPELL: Beginning just before midnight on the full moon, write the full name of your enemy three times in the center of your paper square in red ink. You can also write "MY ENEMY" if you don't know their name. Make the names look like this:

FIRST MIDDLE LAST

FIRST MIDDLE LAST

FIRST MIDDLE LAST

Next, working clockwise, surround the names with a red square and, in each corner and on each side of the square, draw (clockwise) an arrow across the line that points at the names in the center, like this:

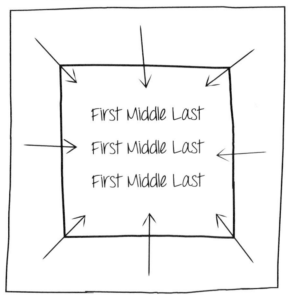

Go outside and heat up your charcoal in a heat-safe grill or firepit. Your charcoal briquettes may or may not already have lighter fluid in them. If not, you might need to add some to get the coals started. While the charcoal heats up, repeat this verbal charm three times, blowing across the coals after each recitation: "(NAME or MY ENEMY), your hands and feet will burn away. (NAME or MY ENEMY), your hands and feet will rot away. What can you do with hands and feet like this? Your hands won't work against me. Your feet won't walk toward me. All of this until the stars above all fade away."

After this, cut out the core in your apple but leave the rest of the fruit intact. There are a number of ways you can do this. You can use a tool specifically for coring fruit, or you can work in the traditional way and heat an iron poker to red on your coals and then drive it through the core of an apple. Either way works just as well, just make sure to enter through the stem side.

Once you have the apple cored, roll up the paper square and slide it into the center of the apple. If you have any identifying materials from your target, you can also roll them up with the paper square before sliding it into the apple. Toss some of your bull nettle leaves and berries onto the coals. Make sure to wear a mask while doing this, and only burn this plant outside, as its smoke can irritate your lungs and might even make you dizzy. Stab the apple onto the end of your knife and hold it over the smoke while you repeat the verbal charm another three times.

Remove the apple from the end of your knife, then finish the ritual by burying the apple in the roots of a honey locust or by piercing the apple onto its thorns. Let the apple and your enemy rot away with the waning moon.

VARIATIONS: If you aren't able to gather bull nettle in the wild, you can substitute this with any other species from the nightshade family or black oak bark (*Quercus velutina*).

BIBLE VERSE: You can replace the verbal charm in the original spell with Isaiah 5:24. "Therefore, as the tongue of fire devours the stubble, and as dry grass sinks down in the flame, so their root will become rotten, and their blossom go up like dust; for they have rejected the instruction of the Lord of hosts, and have despised the word of the Holy One of Israel."

NOTES: The informant who gave me this "rotting away" rite said he always used a goat heart as the container, not an apple. Butchers often sell animal organs at discounted prices in case you would like to work in this way. You can also consider partnering with a local farm to source meats and other animal products in a more humane way. While traditional magic from the old Ozarks does often incorporate items from animals like this, there are many, many other containers that can be used just as effectively. Commonly, potatoes and apples have been used by Ozarkers because they are easily available and are usually a staple of every cabin kitchen.

RITUAL TO SEW UP A SLANDERER'S MOUTH

MAGICAL TIMING: Waning moon; Tuesday; Scorpio

INGREDIENTS:

- Cloth bag with drawstring top, black
- Needle for sewing, new
- Paper square, red, 5 inches by 5 inches
- Pen, black
- Thread, black, enough to sew the paper
- Identifying materials (optional)

SPELL: First, write your enemy's full name (or "MY ENEMY") on your paper square three times in black ink, one on top of the other like this:

FIRST MIDDLE LAST

FIRST MIDDLE LAST

FIRST MIDDLE LAST

Then, fold the paper in half around any identifying materials you have from the target. Make sure the items all fit within the edges of the paper. If you don't have any, that's not a problem. Starting on the bottom, sew up the edge of the paper in a counterclockwise direction until the paper is completely sealed. Cut off any excess thread.

After you finish sewing the paper, add it to your black bag. Remove the drawstring from the bag, then using your thread and needle, sew up the bag's "mouth" while repeating this verbal charm until you are finished: "Your lips be sealed, slanderer! Until the mountains turn to dust and the sea boils! Until the stars fall out of the sky and the world is destroyed!"

Once sewn, cut off any excess thread still attached. At midnight during the waning moon, take and hang the bag in the branches of a black oak tree (*Quercus velutina*) or bury at a four-way crossroads.

VARIATIONS: You can also fill the bag with any appropriate plants before sewing it up. I like to use anything with thorns like common field thistle (*Cirsium* spp.), bull nettle (*Solanum carolinense*), or greenbrier (*Smilax rotundifolia*).

BIBLE VERSE: You can replace the verbal charm in the original spell with Psalm 140:10–12. "Let burning coals fall on them! Let them be flung into pits, no more to rise! Do not let the slanderer be established in the land; let evil speedily hunt down the violent! I know that the Lord maintains the cause of the needy, and executes justice for the poor."

NOTES: In more traditional forms of this ritual, old-timers would have incorporated the tongue of an animal as a stand-in for the slanderer's own tongue. In some cases, the tongue itself would have been split open, filled with identifying materials and malign ingredients, and then sewn up again. In other variations, the tongue would just have been sewn into the bag alongside the other items.

RITUAL TO REVERSE A HEX

MAGICAL TIMING: New moon; Tuesday; Scorpio

INGREDIENTS:

- Bowl or plate
- Lighter or matches
- Paper square, red, 5 inches by 5 inches, or photo of hexer
- Pen, black
- Taper, votive, or jar candle, black

SPELL: At midnight on the new moon, take and write the full name of the one who hexed you (or "MY ENEMY") three times in the center of the paper square like this:

FIRST MIDDLE LAST

FIRST MIDDLE LAST

FIRST MIDDLE LAST

You can also use a printed photo of the person. On the other side of the paper square (or on the back of the photo), write these words: "What's been done, fire undo. What's been made, fire unmake."

Now, hold your paper square or photo so that the words or image are in their regular position. Blow three times onto the paper or photo, visualizing the curse inside you as a black cloud that leaves your body and enters the paper. Then spin the paper or photo counterclockwise while repeating this verbal charm three times: "(NAME or MY ENEMY), I turn you around! I spin you until you are dizzy. Your eyes cannot see me, your ears cannot hear me. Fire undo, fire unmake." After you finish these words, make sure to stop spinning when the words on the paper square or the image in the photo is upside down.

Light your black candle. You can use any candle you'd like, whether it is a taper (of any length), jar, or even a small votive, so long as it is black. If you're using a taper candle, make sure you also have a holder so that it won't fall over during the ritual.

Hold the photo or paper square in the flame of your black candle, then burn completely using a heat-safe bowl or plate. Take any ashes that remain and bury them in the roots of a black oak tree (*Quercus velutina*).

VARIATIONS: You can also do this ritual outside and burn the paper or photo on a bed of hot coals. Try including some of the plants listed in the introduction to this chapter for some added power. When you're finished, collect all the ashes and sprinkle them around a black oak tree (*Quercus velutina*) or throw them into a moving body of water.

BIBLE VERSE: You can replace the verbal charm in the original spell with Psalm 54:3–5. "For the insolent have risen against me, the ruthless seek my life; they do not set God before them. But surely, God is my helper; the Lord is the upholder of my life. He will repay my enemies for their evil. In your faithfulness, put an end to them."

NOTES: This simple yet powerful ritual works on the principle of physically spinning an item as a way of magically reversing a hex. Another traditional Ozark countercharm along these same lines was to take off your shirt or coat and flip it inside out, then put it back on immediately after feeling the presence of a witch or seeing your enemy. Others say that all you need to do is walk backward seven steps and then change your clothes for a hex to be reversed. The old clothes in these countercharms were sometimes washed outside the house as a cleansing measure, or they were burned.

DREAMING

PLANET: Moon

ZODIAC: Aquarius, Pisces

DAY: Monday

COLOR: None

ITEMS:

- Keys
- Knives
- Kyanite crystal
- Quartz crystal

PLANTS:

- Mistletoe, American (*Phoradendron leucarpum*)
- Passionflower (*Passiflora incarnata*)
- Rabbit tobacco (*Pseudognaphalium obtusifolium*)
- Wormwood (*Artemisia absinthium*)
- Yarrow (*Achillea millefolium*)

Dreams have always been a powerful tool for Ozark healers and magical practitioners. For many, dreams show us the hidden nature of reality. Namely, they can let us look into a situation or illness more fully, beyond what our human eyes would be able to see. I've met several healers who still incorporate dreams into their diagnosis methods for all their clients. Usually, the healer first interviews their client and tries to gain as much information about their life and situation as possible. Then they "take it dreaming" with them, meaning they observe their own dreams as providing deeper information and insight about their client. In most cases, the dreaming healers I've met all described lucid dreaming experiences on a regular basis, although they themselves never used that terminology. Being able to recognize that they were dreaming and therefore able to observe and delve deeper at will was seen as a vital skill for the work.

In the old Ozarks, I imagine many healers and magical practitioners worked in the same way. After all, dreaming has been a part of our human experience for as long as we've been human. Dreams were also a way for the common Ozarker to self-diagnose issues and illnesses within their own lives. Manuals about dream symbolism were once popular items in country stores and pharmacies. These common symbols and omens, or what the Ozark people called *tokens*, were sometimes even printed in almanacs and newspapers. With guides like these, ordinary folks could interpret the hidden meaning behind their dreams and even use the symbols as a form of divination. For most people in the Ozarks, this was childish fun at best. Few people ever took these guides seriously. They became almost a household pastime and party favorite, akin to the famous Ouija board being released in the late nineteenth century as a toy and novelty item. Those who did take dreams and other forms of divination seriously were magical practitioners, pious churchgoers, or both, in some cases. While dreams remained an important divination and diagnosis method for healers, they were often denounced as demonic messages from the pulpits. Justification for such work often came from the story of Joseph in the Bible, commanded by his god to interpret the dreams of Pharaoh. As one dreamer told me, "If it was holy for Joseph, why can't it be holy for me?"

DREAM SCHOOLS

Dreams haven't just been used for divination and diagnosis; some Ozark practitioners even claim to have gained the power itself from interactions with otherworldly beings while dreaming. As one healer told me, she attended her "dream school," as she called it, for many years when she was a teenager. Almost every night she would dream about being in a big, old-fashioned schoolhouse, but it was just her and a nice older woman as her teacher. During each session, the woman would teach her something about her gift, whether it was ritual methods, theory, or even what plants to gather and use for medicines. Every morning when she woke up, my informant would write down as much as she could remember from the dream. This continued for years, until one night the dreams stopped and my informant told me she felt like she had "graduated and was ready to take [her] gift out into the world."

This informant's story isn't a rare one, albeit I'd never met—and still haven't met—anyone with such an extensive and elaborate lucid dreaming environment. I'm certain that healers of the past also gained much of their knowledge in the same way, or through simulated dream states brought on through trance or encounters with entheogens, plants containing psychoactive chemicals that can produce altered states of perception or consciousness. As with many areas of Ozark folk magic, this sort of work was often condemned as witchcraft; therefore, few practitioners were ever able to pass down their knowledge.

This is why modern dreamers are so interesting. In many cases, these "dream teachers," when described by healers I've met, have been identified as healers from the old Ozarks. These are sometimes ancestors of the dreamer, identified by the individual themselves from family stories or even photographs. Other times, the dream teacher will identify themselves. In one story I heard, an older man said he often spoke to an old granny woman called Ida in his dreams. He told me that when Ida first introduced herself to him, she said she was from a holler not too far from where he was born and that she had died during the Civil War. She was apparently present at my informant's birth and "read signs on his body," as he described, that pointed to him being a healer one day. Ida often appeared for my informant when he wasn't able to identify the source of a curse or illness, or when he needed a powerful ritual but was having trouble formulating all the proper ingredients and steps.

DANGEROUS DREAMING

Dreaming does come with its own dangers and warnings. Many Ozarkers still believe that the soul can leave the body during dreams. If it can fly out, it can also be prevented from reentering. This can produce a sluggish, "zombie-like" state, described by some Ozark healers as being the result of the spirit and body not being in alignment. In the old days, stories abounded about witches using their powers to invade people's dreams and steal their vital energy or even soul. Or, in some more interesting tales, a person could be "hag ridden." This condition was characterized by waking up feeling like you didn't sleep at all, or with the sensation that you had been running in your sleep all night. Some even claimed to have woken up with scratches and cuts all over their bodies. This was believed to be caused by witches who could snatch out your spirit while you sleep, transform it into an animal (usually a mule or donkey), and then ride it across great distances to their infernal gatherings.

Certain warding objects were hung or placed next to the bed to prevent this from happening. In the Ozarks, these included kitchen sieves, or specialized sieves made from weaving together horsehair. It was believed that a witch had to fly back and forth through each hole in the sieve before they could invade your dreams. This process was said to take so long that they eventually gave up and went off to find an easier victim. Along similar lines, bowls full of salt or mustard seeds were also placed near the bed as a countercharm. The belief was that a witch had to count every grain of salt or every seed before they could harm you.

DREAMING WITH TOOLS

Old skeleton keys are usually used for these rituals and are hung on the wall near where you sleep as a way of magically revealing secrets through your dreams. This ritual is particularly powerful when you suspect someone might be talking or working behind your back and you'd like to reveal their identity. Knives are also used for dreaming in addition to magical healing and are placed under the sleeper's pillow to help magically cut apart nightmares. (They can also be placed underneath the bed if you're like me and would worry about accidently cutting yourself in the night.) The Bible has been used in a similar way; when placed underneath the pillow, it can help prevent nightmares or the intrusion of evil into your dreams.

Many modern practitioners incorporate different crystals and gemstones into their practice. This isn't a modern fad, although crystals used to be much more difficult to acquire in the old days. Using crystals and gemstones for their inherent magical correspondences and qualities is an ancient practice that has permeated many different folk magic traditions. The Ozarks have an abundance of different crystal varieties on account of our cavernous landscape or *karst topography*, where caves are formed from the dissolution of soft limestone rock. Basically, we Ozarkers are standing on top of ground that looks like Swiss cheese. Because of this, many Ozarkers have made good livings from digging up crystals and other precious stones and selling them to tourists. Nowadays, many of these crystals don't stay in the state because they are shipped off to online retailers and metaphysical shops across the country.

One of the most common crystals in the Ozarks, and a much beloved crystal by many hillfolk, is the ordinary quartz crystal. I've met many modern healers and magical practitioners who use quartz in their practice, specifically surrounding dream/trance work as well as divination. In the simplest ritual, a piece of quartz can be kept under the pillow or close beside the sleeper as a way of magically cleansing the dreams, much like an egg could be used to suck illness and evil from the body. The quartz is then cleansed the next morning, usually using spring water and salt, before placing it back under the pillow. I've also met practitioners who specialize in trance or astral work who will hold quartz crystals as a way of grounding themselves during the visions.

Most workers who use quartz, or any crystals really, will always have one or two very special stones, usually ones they themselves found out in the wild. These receive the bulk of their magical focus and are therefore seen as powerful tools that can sometimes even be passed down through family lines.

DREAMING WITH THE FOREST

Plants also play an important role in Ozark dream magic, particularly species that are known sedatives or that have mild psychotropic properties. The most widely used of the dream plants are passionflower (*Passiflora incarnata*), a wonderful native plant and source for passionfruit, and rabbit tobacco, or sweet everlasting (*Pseudognaphalium obtusifolium*). Infusions of passionflower leaves and flowers have long been used by hillfolk as a gentle sedative, nervine, and antispasmodic, which means it can help relieve muscle spasms. Because of this association with relaxation and sleep, passionflower has also been used to aid with magical dreaming as well as astral travel through trance. Rabbit tobacco, while not containing any specific sedative properties, can be added to hot water to create a pleasant, relaxing tea that aids in sleeping as well as stomachaches, heartburn, headaches, and even asthma. Smoke from burning rabbit tobacco is said to be able to help with revelatory trance experiences as well as help cleanse the area of illness and evil entities.

Yarrow (*Achillea millefolium*) has also been traditionally used to help aid in magical dreaming. Usually yarrow and passionflower are mixed, either as an infusion that is drank or as a smoke that is inhaled during trance rituals. Yarrow has many magical and medicinal uses, but one is as a mild sedative and nervine derived from the thujone contained in the plant. This chemical compound also contributes to the properties of *Artemisia* species like wormwood and mugwort, also used in similar applications as a dream- and trance-inducing plant. The thujone contained in yarrow is much lower than that of wormwood, so it's often recommended for beginners. Caution should be taken when using essential oils from any thujone-containing plants. The chemical compound is concentrated in the essential oil, so you can easily use too much if applied directly to the skin. The essential oil should never be consumed orally. In high or concentrated amounts, thujone poisoning can lead to severe seizures, muscle spasms, and hallucinations. This is really only a risk when using essential oils or alcohol tinctures of thujone-containing plants, both of which yield a concentrated end product. Traditional methods involving yarrow and stone mint, or common dittany (*Cunila origanoides*), which also contains trace amounts of thujone), use them either in oils and salves that are applied to the skin, allowing the chemical compounds to gently absorb through the pores, or as infusions which aren't able to extract enough of the chemical compounds to risk poisoning.

Many modern workers I've met have reached far back into their own European ancestry to revive traditional uses surrounding wormwood (*Artemisia absinthium*) and common mugwort (*Artemisia vulgaris*). Both of these plants have been common features of many European and Eurasian folk traditions for centuries. Because of their chemical makeup and thujone content, they can both be used to help induce dreaming experiences, specifically lucid dreaming, as well as in trance or astral travel sessions. I myself use infusions of wormwood whenever I want to dream up magical solutions for my clients.

While not used internally, mistletoe also has deep associations with dreaming and trance work, specifically in aiding with revelatory dreams. American mistletoe (*Phoradendron leucarpum*) is commonly used, although our ancestors who brought many of these magical traditions would have used the European mistletoe (*Viscum album*), a far less toxic variety. American mistletoe is very toxic when ingested, and smoke from burning the plant can irritate the lungs and throat. Take caution when using and handling the plant. Ozarkers have used mistletoe more as a magical object and ingredient than as a medicine. For dreamers, it has been hung up above the bed to induce magical dreams, specifically dreams related to revealing the identity of your enemies or someone who has wronged you. Because of its long associations with the sun and light, mistletoe can be used in any dream ritual focusing on revealing the truth or shedding light on something hidden in the shadows. Traditionally, Ozarkers gather their mistletoe on the Winter Solstice following the ancient pan-European tradition. According to hillfolk belief, the mistletoe takes the last bit of sunlight on the darkest day of the year and stores it inside its leaves and berries. We can benefit from this light by bringing branches of mistletoe inside our homes and hanging them over doorways so that the light can shower down on anyone who passes underneath. There is a belief, though, that mistletoe should only be kept inside the house during the twelve days of Christmas (December 25–January 5) and should be removed and burned on "Old Christmas," or Epiphany, January 6.

RITUAL TO AID WITH MAGICAL DREAMING

MAGICAL TIMING: Full moon; Thursday; Pisces

INGREDIENTS:

- Knife
- Paper square, white, 4 inches by 4 inches
- Passionflower leaves, dried (*Passiflora incarnata*)
- Pen, any color
- Water
- Yarrow flowers, dried (*Achillea millefolium*)

CAUTIONS: Do not ingest passionflower or yarrow while you are pregnant.

SPELL: On the night of the full moon, begin this ritual by drawing this symbol on your paper square using any color of ink you choose:

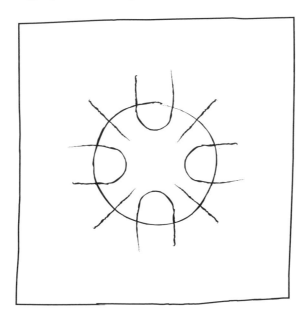

Next, prepare your dreaming infusion. Bring a cup of water to boil and let it set for a minute to reduce the temperature slightly. Add a teaspoon each of dried and crushed passionflower leaves and yarrow flowers. (If you are wild harvesting your plants, make sure to gather them from areas that aren't sprayed with harmful chemicals or around roadsides, where they can absorb exhaust from vehicles.) Stir the infusion with the blade of your knife clockwise three times, then counterclockwise three times.

Let your infusion steep for three to five minutes. Strain, then blow across the surface of the liquid three times. After each time, repeat this verbal charm: "As a flower blooms, let my dreams bloom tonight. Let my eyes see and my ears hear. As a flower is sweet, let my dreams be sweet tonight. Let my eyes see and my ears hear."

Drink the tea, then place the paper square underneath your pillow and go to sleep.

VARIATIONS: One variation I was given was for dreaming of a specific theme or person. In this case, write the full name of the one you want to dream about three times on the side of the paper square that does not contain the drawing, like this:

FIRST MIDDLE LAST

FIRST MIDDLE LAST

FIRST MIDDLE LAST

You can also place a photo of them alongside the square underneath your pillow. If you want to influence your dream to go in a certain direction, draw pictures of the symbols you would like to enter your dreams on the blank side of the paper square, and it's said they will manifest for you.

BIBLE VERSE: You can replace the verbal charm in the original spell with Joel 2:28. "Then afterward I will pour out my spirit on all flesh; your sons and your daughters shall prophesy, your old men shall dream dreams, and your young men shall see visions."

NOTES: This spell was given to me by an Ozark witch who used this formula often to be able to dream of client illnesses and hexes. She believed that the dreams that appeared after performing this ritual would give her insights into the real causes behind certain symptoms or situations. For that reason, it's wise to keep a notepad or voice recorder near your bed to be able to capture any of these magical dreams before you forget them.

RITUAL TO DREAM OF YOUR TRUE LOVE

MAGICAL TIMING: Full moon; Friday; Taurus

INGREDIENTS:

- Heatproof bowl or cup
- Honey
- Mint sprig, fresh or dried
- Redbud flowers, fresh or dried (*Cercis canadensis*)
- Water

SPELL: Do this ritual on the full moon, about an hour before you go to sleep. Take and heat one cup of water to boiling, then let it cool slightly in a heatproof bowl or cup. Add a tablespoon of redbud flowers, then let it steep for about three minutes. (Make sure if you are wild harvesting your plants that you gather them from areas that aren't sprayed with harmful chemicals or around roadsides, where they can absorb exhaust from vehicles.)

Once steeped, strain off the flowers and then stir clockwise with the sprig of mint. Repeat this verbal charm three times while stirring: "A fire on the mountain grows and grows. I walk through smoke, I walk through darkness, I walk through flames. Light at my feet, mirror in front. I look and see myself. I look and in the fiery light I see my heart's love." Add a teaspoon of honey to the tea, then drink.

It's believed that because of this spell, a mirror will appear in your dream. Look in this mirror and your true love will show themselves to you.

VARIATIONS: Other edible flowers have also been used in similar rituals as this one. You can easily substitute violets, rose petals, or calendula, as long as the flower is safe to consume. Repeat the original ritual with your flower of choice. If you don't have a sprig of mint available, you can stir the tea with a wooden spoon or even a bamboo chopstick; anything will work as long as it isn't made of metal.

BIBLE VERSE: You can replace the verbal charm in the original spell with Song of Solomon 5:2. "I slept, but my heart was awake. Listen! My beloved is knocking. 'Open to me, my sister, my love, my dove, my perfect one; for my head is wet with dew, my locks with the drops of the night.'"

NOTES: This is one of many Ozark rituals for dreaming of your true love. Others involve more complicated measures, like going to bed with salt in your mouth. Supposedly, if you do this, the first person to appear in your dream will be the one you marry. Another ritual is washing your face with dew collected on the morning of May 1 (May Day) or the Summer Solstice just before you go to bed to induce a divinatory dream. It's said that in the dream you will be invited to a natural spring to bathe; whoever is also in the spring with you will be your true love. Because marriage was such an important part of hillfolk life, creative young people came up with a variety of divination methods over the years to help speed up the process a little bit.

A KEY TO REVEAL THE TRUTH

MAGICAL TIMING: Full moon; Wednesday; Gemini

INGREDIENTS:

- 1 key
- Knife
- Large bowl
- 1 nail, new
- Paper square, white, 4 inches by 4 inches
- String
- Water
- Yarrow flowers, dried (*Achillea millefolium*)

SPELL: Gather your items, then fill a large bowl with water. Traditionally this would be spring water taken from inside a cave where the sun cannot touch it, but you can also use ordinary tap water. Take the paper square in one hand and the new nail in the other, then poke five holes in the paper square in this shape:

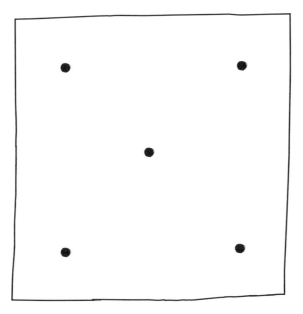

Next, wrap or fold the paper around your key. You can tie it with some string if you need to. Unlike the nail, this can be any key; there aren't any taboos surrounding whether or not it should be new. Those I've met who perform ritual dreaming like this on a regular basis have a key they use only for this purpose, and many choose old skeleton keys for aesthetic purposes.

Put the paper and key in the bowl of water along with a good-sized clump of yarrow flowers. Take your knife and stir the water clockwise while repeating this verbal charm three times: "In the old, old house there's an old, old lock. That old, old lock's never been unlocked before. But now in the old, old house there's an old, old key for the old, old lock. When I hold the old, old key in my hand the old, old lock will open."

When you've repeated the charm three times, take the bowl outside and leave it under the full moon. You'll want to do this on a clear night. Make sure that apart from tree cover, the bowl is completely out in the open. Leave the bowl overnight.

In the morning, pour the water from the bowl on a nearby tree. Unwrap the key and bury the paper where you poured out the water. Finally, tie a length of string onto the key, then keep it in a secret place. Whenever you have a situation you can't quite figure out, or some truth in your life that needs to be illuminated, wear the key around your neck when you go to sleep, especially on full moon nights. Repeat the verbal charm as you fall asleep, and the truth will be revealed in your dreams.

VARIATIONS: None

BIBLE VERSE: You can replace the verbal charm in the original spell with Matthew 16:19. *"I will give you the keys of the kingdom of heaven, and whatever you bind on earth will be bound in heaven, and whatever you loose on earth will be loosed in heaven."*

NOTES: Keys have also been used as items for creating magical pendulums. In this case, a string would be tied to the ring end of the key and then suspended over a person's body or a chart that marked out certain options, almost like a Ouija board. When used directly with a patient, the healer looked for specific movements of the pendulum that might indicate where illnesses or hexes were hidden underneath the skin.

RITUAL TO DREAM WITH WORMWOOD

MAGICAL TIMING: Full moon; Thursday; Pisces

INGREDIENTS:

- Honey
- Offering mixture for spirits: equal parts oats, whole barley, and cornmeal
- Ribbon or strip of cloth, blue, 3 feet
- Water or milk
- Wormwood leaves, fresh or dried (*Artemisia absinthium*)

CAUTIONS: Do not consume wormwood when you are pregnant. Wormwood does contain the chemical thujone, which in high or concentrated amounts can cause hallucinations, delirium, and muscle spasms. Do not use tinctures or extracts of wormwood internally for this reason. The amounts used in this infusion are generally considered safe for consumption.

SPELL: Part of this ritual will involve petitioning the spirit of wormwood to aid you in your work. I highly recommend growing your own wormwood. Otherwise, the dried foliage can be easily purchased online or at your local herb and magic retailer. If you are wild harvesting your plants, make sure to gather them from areas that aren't sprayed with harmful chemicals or around roadsides, where they can absorb exhaust from vehicles. If you do have a plant of your own, on the night you would like to perform this spell, begin by taking some of your offering mixture and sprinkling it clockwise around your wormwood plant. Then tie a blue ribbon or strip of cloth either around the pot holding the wormwood or, if it's in the ground, loosely around the base of the plant.

Once that's finished, make your wormwood tea. Heat one cup of water or milk to boiling and let it cool slightly. Add a teaspoon of wormwood herb and let this steep for about five minutes. Strain the plant matter from the liquid. Add some honey and stir to incorporate.

Once the tea has cooled, stir in a clockwise direction with the forefinger of your right hand while repeating this verbal charm three times: "Mother wormwood, up from the ground. Up and up, she makes a tree. I climb the tree, so high, so high. Its branches wide, its branches tall. Mother wormwood in the sky. Up and up, she makes a tree. I climb the tree to heaven's gate. Now visions come, by Mother's grace."

Drink this tea before you go to sleep for the night. It's believed that the dreams you have during this ritual will be able to guide you in many areas of life, healing, magic, and even love.

VARIATIONS: You can also use wormwood as a smoke instead of making the tea. In this ritual, you will put some of the dried herb onto an incense charcoal and let the smoke fill the room where you will be sleeping. Repeat the verbal charm three times over the burning wormwood. The smoke can be quite strong, so I recommend only burning a small amount and extinguishing the charcoal before going to sleep.

If you don't want to use the smoke, you can also do this with steam by pouring boiling water over some of the fresh or dried herb. Repeat the verbal charm three times while breathing in the steam, then go to sleep with the steaming bowl still near your bed.

BIBLE VERSE: You can replace the verbal charm in the original spell with Psalm 43:3–4. "O send out your light and your truth; let them lead me; let them bring me to your holy hill and to your dwelling. Then I will go to the altar of God, to God my exceeding joy; and I will praise you with the harp, O God, my God."

NOTES: Wormwood isn't native to the Ozarks, but has been used by hillfolk over the years, mostly medicinally. Its name is derived from its use as a vermifuge, or a medicine that will aid in killing internal parasites. Trance and dreaming uses of the plant seem to be a modern development, in particular one that has formed through contact with European witch traditions and practices. I myself love using the plant, as the bulk of my ancient Celtic, German, and Scandinavian ancestors would have certainly used it in medicines and rituals.

A MISTLETOE AMULET TO REVEAL YOUR ENEMY

MAGICAL TIMING: Full moon; Wednesday (Gemini) or Thursday (Pisces)

INGREDIENTS:

- Cloth bag with drawstring top, white or blue
- Cloth strip or bandana, blue, for a blindfold
- Juniper essential oil or gin
- Incense charcoal and burner, with metal tongs
- Lighter or matches
- Mistletoe sprig (*Phoradendron leucarpum*)
- Paper square, white, 5 inches by 5 inches
- Pen, blue
- Red cedar berries, fresh or dried (*Juniperus virginiana*), or dried juniper berries (*Juniperus communis*)
- String, blue, 3 feet

CAUTIONS: While European mistletoe (*Viscum album*) has traditionally been used internally by herbalists, *this species is very rare in the US*. American mistletoe (*Phoradendron leucarpum*) can be toxic if ingested, especially the berries. Do not consume any part of the plant. Smoke from burning American mistletoe can also irritate the lungs and esophagus. Be sure to wear gloves when gathering and working with the fresh foliage. Dried mistletoe is relatively inert, but the fresh sap can cause contact dermatitis where it comes into contact with the skin.

SPELL: Begin by drawing this symbol on one side of your paper square in blue ink:

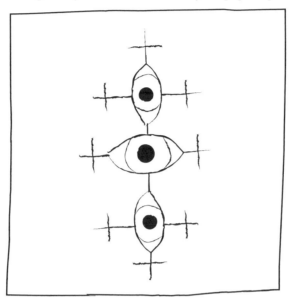

Next, fold your paper square to the size of your cloth bag, then wrap the paper in blue string and tie with three knots. Put the paper inside the bag along with your sprig of mistletoe and a pinch of red cedar berries or crushed juniper berries. Pull the top of the bag closed and seal with three knots.

After your bag is made, light your incense charcoal by holding it in the flame from a lighter or matches using metal tongs. Once hot, add some red cedar or crushed juniper berries. Spin your bag through this smoke clockwise seven times. Once finished, take your strip of blue cloth or blue bandana and tie it over your eyes so that you can't see anything. Recite this verbal charm three times while holding the bag in your hands at eye level: "Hidden truth, secrets out of sight, mistletoe let my eyes be opened. Mistletoe, let your light illuminate me." When you've repeated the charm three times, untie your blindfold.

Your mistletoe bag can be hung up near your bed or even worn while you sleep. When you want the hidden truth behind a situation or person to be revealed in your dreams, hold the bag at eye level and repeat the verbal charm three times. Do this immediately before going to sleep.

Anoint your bag with three drops of gin or juniper essential oil on the new and full moon to recharge.

VARIATIONS: If you don't have access to mistletoe, you can also perform this ritual using other plants associated with the second sight, dreaming, and visions. Yarrow (*Achillea millefolium*) is a very good choice, as is cinquefoil or five-finger grass (*Potentilla* spp.). In a pinch, you can also just use the red cedar or juniper berries. In all cases, make sure you change the plant invoked in the verbal charm to the one you are using.

BIBLE VERSE: You can replace the verbal charm in the original spell with Psalm 64:1–4. "Hear my voice, O God, in my complaint; preserve my life from the dread enemy. Hide me from the secret plots of the wicked, from the scheming of evildoers, who whet their tongues like swords, who aim bitter words like arrows, shooting from ambush at the blameless; they shoot suddenly and without fear."

NOTES: The most powerful mistletoe used in rituals like this is gathered on the Winter Solstice. Amongst many Ozark witches and healers, mistletoe is never cut from its tree, but instead pulled. And because the plant is seen as an intermediary between the worlds, mistletoe is never allowed to touch the ground.

RITUAL TO DREAM OF YOUR ANCESTORS USING RABBIT TOBACCO

MAGICAL TIMING: Full moon; Monday; Cancer

INGREDIENTS:

- Ancestor foods and drinks (see Notes section)
- Incense charcoal and burner, with metal tongs
- Lighter or matches
- Paper square, white, 3 inches by 3 inches
- Pen, blue
- Rabbit tobacco leaves and/or flowers, dried (*Pseudognaphalium obtusifolium*)

SPELL: First, put out your ancestor food and drink offerings. Place these on or near your home altar/shrine if you have one. If you don't, you can create a simple shrine for this spell using a small table or even a foldable TV tray that is covered with a white cloth. Many ancestor altars are also topped with family items and other personal items, but these are not necessary for this spell. Since you will be dreaming in this ritual, you can also place these offerings near or even underneath your bed. Be sure to keep your offerings out of reach of any nosy pets you might have in your home.

The point of the offerings is to welcome any of your ancestors to the space to guide you in your dreams. These ancestors could be ones you knew in life and already work with as guiding spirits. It's possible that you will also encounter your ancestors for the first time. It's important to know that you don't have to invite in any ancestors who might have caused you trauma in life or who were known to be not-so-great people. While it's important to hold space for these ancestors to heal, your safety and comfort is of utmost importance. The verbal charm for this ritual is specifically formulated to welcome in those ancestors who wish us well on our journey while also creating a magical boundary that spirits who need to do some growing can't cross.

After your food and drink offerings are placed, draw this symbol on your paper square in blue ink. It represents the crossroads whereby the ancestors might enter our world, as well as our own eyes that will be blessed to see them in our dreams:

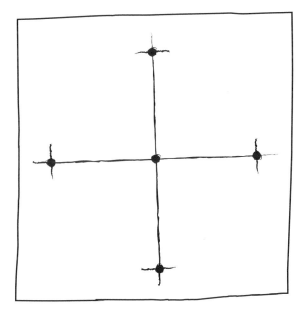

When you're ready to go to sleep, light your charcoal by holding it in the flame from a lighter or matches, making sure to also use metal tongs as the coal will quickly get hot. Next, take some rabbit tobacco and place it on the paper square, then place all of that on the charcoal and let the smoke rise up around you. Repeat this verbal charm three times while wafting the smoke over your head using your cupped hands: "Family of my blood and work, I welcome you to this feast. Take your fill of food and drink and be at peace, be satisfied. Bring me your words of wisdom in dreams and visions. Guide me with your lamps and let all obstacles be removed from my path. Let only those who wish me well, who want to see me happy, healthy, and prosperous, enter this place. Let only those with words of peace and cleansing guide my dreams tonight."

Make sure your incense charcoal is extinguished or in a safe place where it can burn out on its own, then go to sleep and dream.

VARIATIONS: While the main ingredient in this spell is the native plant rabbit tobacco, or sweet everlasting, you can also use other plants with similar correspondences including yarrow (*Achillea millefolium*), mugwort (*Artemisia vulgaris*), wormwood (*Artemisia absinthium*), sweetgum (*Liquidambar styraciflua*), and even red cedar (*Juniperus virginiana*) or common juniper (*Juniperus communis*).

BIBLE VERSE: You can replace the verbal charm in the original spell with Genesis 28:12–14. "And he dreamed that there was a ladder set up on the earth, the top of it reaching to heaven; and the angels of God were ascending and descending on it. And the Lord stood beside him and said, 'I am the Lord, the God of Abraham your father and the God of Isaac; the land on which you lie I will give to you and to your offspring; and your offspring shall be like the dust of the earth, and you shall spread abroad to the west and to the east and to the north and to the south; and all the families of the earth shall be blessed in you and in your offspring.'"

NOTES: On the subject of ancestor food and drink offerings, there are a couple options. These include providing specific food and drink items your known ancestors would have enjoyed, or providing general offerings for ancestors who you might not yet know or who haven't told you about any of their preferences. Specific offerings can be for as many ancestors as you would like to contact, or they could be for a select few who were and still are very important to your life and work. I always suggest starting off small and as close to you as you can get. This includes your immediate family as well as grandparents, aunts, uncles, and cousins. You might not know if any ancestors want to get in touch with you. In this case, just provide some general food and drink offerings.

General offerings for ancestors, from the Ozark context, include grains like oats, barley, and cornmeal, as well as any food items made from these (cornbread or barley cakes, for instance). General ancestor drinks include black tea (hot or cold, unsweet or sweetened), coffee (black or with milk), flavored sodas, and "soft" alcohols like beer, wine, or mead. Whiskey and moonshine are also common Ozark drink offerings, but I find they sometimes unnerve ancestors who might have been teetotalers.

DIVINATION

PLANET: Mercury

ZODIAC: Gemini, Cancer, Sagittarius, Pisces

DAY: Wednesday

COLOR: Blue

ITEMS:

- Blue bottles
- Corn kernels, beans, and buttons
- Dowsing rods
- Holed objects (stones, roots, and bones)
- Quartz crystal

PLANTS:

- Five-finger grass, cinquefoil (*Potentilla* spp.)
- Mugwort (*Artemisia vulgaris*)
- Red cedar (*Juniperus virginiana*)
- Spicebush (*Lindera benzoin*)
- Tobacco (*Nicotiana tabacum*), or "wild tobacco" (*N. rustica*)
- Yarrow (*Achillea millefolium*)

Divination has long been an important part of Ozark folk magic. For many healers, divining was the most common form of diagnosis for magical illnesses and hexes. Countless methods have been used, many of which were passed through family lines and are still around today. These methods could include anything from reading cards to using a pendulum or dowsing rod and many more crazy and interesting techniques in between. Divination was one way for Ozark magical practitioners to remain "in tune" with their own gift, so to speak, or the presence of their guiding spirits, ancestors, or even divine entities. Divination has always been about letting go of control and relying upon some outside force in the universe to reveal an answer, sometimes to questions you didn't even know you asked. This trust has always been vital to the Ozark healer's work and their interaction with the community around them. The healer trusts their guides and gifts; likewise, the community puts their trust in the healer that they won't trick them or lead them astray.

Yet for many old Ozarkers, divination was akin to witchcraft and therefore seen as the devil's work. These folks used the Bible to justify their condemnation, specifically Deuteronomy 18:9–11, verses I myself heard growing up in the church: "When you come into the land that the Lord your God is giving you, you must not learn to imitate the abhorrent practices of those nations. No one shall be found among you who makes a son or daughter pass through fire, or who practices divination, or is a soothsayer, or an augur, or a sorcerer, or one who casts spells, or who consults ghosts or spirits, or who seeks oracles from the dead." These three verses allowed for a whole lot of practices to be covered under the same condemnation and were used to accuse many innocent Ozark people of witchcraft.

Despite these condemnations, consulting oracles and fortune-tellers were once popular activities amongst common folk across the area. Divinatory methods abound, as Vance Randolph and Mary Parler's vast folklore collections can attest to. Both collected hundreds of methods, most of which specifically related to love or finding a spouse. This was a very important subject for hillfolk, who often married young and out of necessity. The risks of becoming an "old maid" were very real and very present for Ozarkers. Not having a family meant no workers on the farm and, more importantly, no one to carry on your legacy. The most famous of the love divinations has to be the dumb supper, which has been transformed over the years into divination for spirits of the dead, but the original intention was identifying your future spouse.

FORESEEING YOUR TRUE LOVE

The dumb supper ritual is a complex and interesting one. It usually involves a group of girls or young women, at most four. As soon as the girls arrive at the house where the dumb supper is to be held, they immediately cease speaking. The entire ritual is performed in silence. They each silently help with the cooking, which is usually something simple like buttered toast or cornbread. Each takes a serving of the meal and puts it on their own plate, then sits down at the dining table in an assigned spot marked with their name.

Next to each person is an empty seat and place setting. Each girl puts some of the meal onto the empty plate next to them. The lights are then lowered in the room save for a single candle in the center of the dining table. Then all of the windows and doors in the house are opened, usually by the girl who lives in the home. Once she returns, each of the participants lower their heads. In some cases, I've been told their eyes should be closed; in others I've been told they should be open.

At this point shades, or spectral images, of each girl's future spouse enter the room and sit next to the one they will marry. The girls can now look beside them and see who they can recognize. Of course, there's always a chance no shade will appear next to one of the girls. This is a sure sign the poor child won't ever marry. Others might receive a shadowy, unidentifiable figure, which is interpreted as a terrible omen that the girl will sadly die before marrying.

The dumb supper is just one of many love divinations in the Ozarks, remembered in anecdotes and fireside stories because of its elaborate ritual. Most of these old divinations have unfortunately died out over the years. One simple ritual that is still practiced occasionally involves bending over—but not breaking—the flower stalk of the mullein plant (*Verbascum thapsus*) toward your love's house. If the stalk grows straight again, it's a sign the other person also loves you. If it remains bent, or even dies, it's a sign to move on.

OZARK DIVINATION TRADITIONS

Today, we live in a time when more and more people are able to freely and openly practice their beliefs as they want to without fear of repercussion. We've still got a long way to go in the Ozarks to ensure this right for *everyone* and not just those in the more developed areas. Traditional divination methods are still an active part of many people's practice. I'd even say more Ozark practitioners have incorporated various methods of divination than ever before. This is mostly because of the availability of tarot and oracle decks today.

As with most other areas of Ozark folk magic, hillfolk have long been resourceful and creative in their forms of divination. Some Ozarkers learned how to read other things like ordinary playing cards, coins, and buttons or more natural items like kernels of corn, pebbles, or cut sticks. Some even took up more ancient forms of divination, like reading omens in the patterns of flying birds (augury), reading signs in the placenta right after giving birth (amniomancy), using divining rods or pendulums (dowsing), or turning to random verses/passages in a book as a form of divination (bibliomancy). Methods abound in the Ozarks, and it seems like every healer and practitioner today has their own preferred form of magical divination.

Traditional Ozark methods of divination rarely included the use of tarot or playing cards, which is why I've left these methods out of my listing at the beginning of this chapter. Methods were based much more in the natural world and observing certain "tokens" or signs. At the most basic level, the forest itself could be observed by someone skilled in recognizing these tokens. The movement of birds, the wind blowing through the leaves, or the calls of certain animals and insects could all point to very specific answers for someone with the gift.

Practitioners and healers also had many household rituals for divination. One common method involved dropping grains or seeds onto hot coals and observing how they popped or moved as an answer to a question. Smoke was also observed in a similar way, specifically smoke from red cedar or tobacco. In one smoke ritual I observed, the healer took a coal out of his fireplace and rolled it into a cast-iron skillet. Once the coal was situated, he dropped some crushed tobacco leaves onto the coal, then we watched as a still, thin stream of smoke went straight up into the air. "That means all is okay," he said, pointing to the stream. Then he said the name of a client he was working with and the smoke stream suddenly began flitting and moving around as if there was a breeze blowing, but no air was moving through the cabin. "That means all is not okay," the healer said. Traditional rituals involving tobacco, like this one, were most likely developed through interactions with Indigenous people in Appalachia.

Dowsing using rods or pendulums has also been a popular divination method of the past and present. Water dowsers—or "witch wigglers," as they're often called in the Ozarks—were once important members of the community because of their ability to locate underground sources of water for wells without needing to dig through the rocky Ozark soil. Dowsers didn't always just use their gift to find water, though. There were also dowsers for dead bodies, particularly important for genealogy enthusiasts trying to locate lost cemeteries, and even dowsers for buried treasure. These were often very popular but the least successful in their practice.

Dowsing rods traditionally came in two shapes and were usually made of witch hazel branches. Nowadays, they also come in metal. One shape for a dowsing rod was the letter L. Two of these Ls would be used, with the short end of each held in each of the dowser's hands. The long ends would be kept apart from each other, but when they naturally crossed it was seen as a confirmation of whatever question the dowser was holding in their mind. The other shape was the Y, where each hand held a different branch on the top of the Y shape, with the long, single end facing outward. When the long end dropped toward the ground of its own accord, this was taken as a confirmation of the question asked.

Healers also used dowsing methods in their work, particularly using pendulums. A string would be tied to a hole stone, already considered a sacred object in its own right, and then the pendulum would be steadied and held above a patient as they lay flat on a bed. The pendulum would be slowly and steadily moved through the air just above the patient's body from head to toe. When the rock started moving, it was taken as a sign that there was some illness or hex sitting in that spot. Many healers still use this method today, and they all seem to have different ways of interpreting the movements of the pendulum, whether it's clockwise or counterclockwise or side to side. In a similar method, a spicebush leaf would be suspended on top of spring water in a bowl, then the directions it spun would be observed as answers to certain questions.

Magical tools that the healer could see through, like blue glass bottles and quartz crystals, were also commonly used as ways for divining illness. I've observed examples of modern practitioners using both of these traditional methods. In one case, the healer had a special blue bottle that they filled with spring water and then brought to the bedside of their patient. They then lit a candle and held it above the person at certain points on their body while looking through the blue glass bottle. They explained to me after the ritual that they observed the way the candlelight spread out at certain points. If there was some sickness or curse at that spot in the body, the light wouldn't spread out as much and would look "dull" or dim.

Quartz crystal, specifically, and clear crystals in general have all been used by Ozark healers and witches to help aid with their own human vision. One practitioner I met had a large, completely clear quartz tip she would gaze through when working with a patient. She told me that she was able to see the exact location of "darkness" inside her patients that she could then remove using various techniques. Others have reported seeing certain colors surrounding people while gazing through crystals like these. As with other systems that seek to observe colors in a person's aura, each color corresponds to a certain gift or deficiency, although a standard meaning for these colors is far from present amongst Ozarkers who use this method.

As in many other ancient divination methods, patterns were also observed by Ozark healers and magical practitioners as providing necessary answers. Specifically, it was patterns observed by dropping a handful of corn kernels, beans, or even buttons onto a flat surface. Much like observing the shapes made by constellations in the sky, certain groupings or shapes made by these objects could point the observer toward a certain answer. Amongst modern practitioners it's become popular to pair this method with a specialized mat or board that displays certain fixed shapes, symbols, or even letters and numbers similar to the Ouija board. The corn kernels or beans then point to these fixed symbols rather than making their own for observation. Also, through interactions with Southern Rootwork, Conjure, and Hoodoo, many practitioners have made sets of "throwing bones" and charms for themselves. These often include animal bones, teeth, and claws, as well as other charms and curios. Each has its own specific meaning and a variable interpretation based on its proximity to other objects when thrown.

Modern divination methods—like using tarot, playing cards, oracle decks, and even sets of Viking runes—are quickly replacing more traditional methods amongst practitioners today. While I certainly advocate for trying to preserve these more ancient methods, I also recognize the need to evolve in our practice and traditions as well. Divination techniques like the tarot might actually be better and more accurate than the ones passed down from the old-timers. In this chapter I will provide some of the more traditional divination methods that you can incorporate into your own practice, but it's important to explore what works best for you, not what seems most "traditional." That might mean looking to your trusty ol' tarot deck instead of an Ozark method, and that's all right! Your power is your own; your practice is your own. You might find that the divination methods you've used in the past are not ones you want to continue using years down the road. Or you might be like me and choose to use a variety of methods, both traditional and modern, depending upon the client and situation at hand.

MAKING A HOLE STONE PENDULUM

MAGICAL TIMING: New moon to full moon; Wednesday; Gemini or Pisces

INGREDIENTS:

- Five-finger grass leaves, dried (*Potentilla* spp.)
- Gin or a water infusion made from red cedar or juniper berries
- Hole stone
- Incense charcoal and burner, with metal tongs
- Knife
- Lighter or matches
- Mugwort leaves, dried (*Artemisia vulgaris*)
- Silver bowl or silver item
- String, blue
- Yarrow flowers, dried (*Achillea millefolium*)

SPELL: Begin this ritual on the new moon. The best magical timing is to have your end point fall on a full moon in Gemini or Pisces.

Start by making your pendulum, which consists of a hole stone large enough to weigh down the string but not so large that it is difficult to hold. Tie one end of the blue string through the hole, then knot three times. You can choose any length you'd like, but I usually make my pendulums about a foot long so that they aren't cumbersome to deal with during rituals. You don't want a bunch of string getting in the way, nor do you want so little string that observing the motion of the pendulum becomes difficult.

Next, place your pendulum in a silver bowl or a regular bowl with a silver item like a ring, chain, or coin added so that it is touching the pendulum. Around the pendulum, also in the bowl, sprinkle a mixture of five-finger grass, mugwort, and yarrow in a clockwise direction.

After this, light your charcoal by holding it in the flame from a lighter or matches. Make sure to use metal tongs, as the coal will quickly get hot. Once hot, sprinkle on some more of your herb mixture. While the smoke rises, repeat this verbal charm over your bowl and pendulum three times: "Veil that's closed, now be opened. Holey stone, let me see. Holey stone, speak loud and true. Holey stone, be a firm friend until one of us passes away." Cut through the air with your knife in a cross shape (up to down, then left to right) after each recitation.

After completing the verbal charm and cutting motion, blow across your pendulum three times, then place it somewhere safe for the full duration of the waxing moon. Each day, repeat the same verbal charm and cutting motion three times, making sure to blow across the pendulum after each recitation. On the full moon, repeat the charm and blowing ritual, then anoint the stone with gin or a water infusion made from red cedar or juniper berries.

You can take the herbs that were in the bowl and either save them to burn whenever you work with your pendulum, or you can sprinkle them around an oak tree outside. Anoint the pendulum with gin (or your infusion) every new and full moon to recharge.

VARIATIONS:

- If you're sensitive to smoke, you can always make a blessing spray instead. Follow the general recipe listed in the book's introduction and use five-finger grass, mugwort, and yarrow as your plants. You can also add a few drops of juniper or camphor essential oil to your spray for added fragrance and magical benefit. Where the original ritual calls for smoke, you can instead use this spray. You can also use it to recharge your pendulum every new and full moon.

- You can also use this ritual for blessing a purchased pendulum made from any material. Many modern pendulums are made from crystal or even precious metals and can be purchased to correspond specifically to the work you are focusing on.

BIBLE VERSE: You can replace the verbal charm in the original spell with Revelation 19:11–13. "Then I saw heaven opened, and there was a white horse! Its rider is called Faithful and True, and in righteousness he judges and makes war. His eyes are like a flame of fire, and on his head are many diadems; and he has a name inscribed that no one knows but himself. He is clothed in a robe dipped in blood, and his name is called The Word of God."

NOTES:

- Ozark pendulums have come in a variety of shapes, sizes, and materials. Hole stones are the most common because of their status as a sacred object anyway, as well as because of the convenient hole that can easily be attached to a string. While many modern healers and magical practitioners will keep tools like these as constant companions in their work, I have met some who choose instead to make a new pendulum each time this sort of divination is called upon for a client. One man I met only used this method of divination in serious cases of magical illness. Each time he determined there was a need for the pendulum, he would go out to a creek near his house and hunt for a new hole stone. Sometimes it would take him hours to find one; other times a hole stone would pop out almost immediately. He judged the effectiveness of the work at hand partially on how easy it was to find a hole stone for his pendulum. After all rituals were completed for his client, he would "lay the stone to rest," as he said, on a bookshelf in his home where it would join many others in a sort of retirement.

- The cross shape that is made with the knife might remind us of the Christian cross, and for some it still holds this symbolism, but for many other Ozark healers the cross is an ancient symbol connected to the crossroads, the four directions, and the sun. Imagine as you make the cross with the knife that you are drawing in power and magic from the four directions and sealing it in the work at hand. If you're still uncomfortable making this shape, you can instead make a clockwise circle with the blade three times.

RITUAL FOR DIVINATION USING FIRE

MAGICAL TIMING: Full moon; Thursday; Sagittarius

INGREDIENTS:

- Beer
- Bread
- Cast-iron skillet or portable grill

- Charcoal briquettes

- Grain mixture: equal parts whole barley, spelt, and steel-cut oats

- Lighter or matches

- Red cedar leaves and/or berries (*Juniperus virginiana*)

SPELL: Since this spell will produce a not-so-pleasant smelling smoke, I recommend divining with fire outside, preferably at night underneath the full moon. I also recommend having a notebook on hand when you do this ritual, or better yet, a voice recorder that you can use to quickly record your questions and thoughts during the session. Come up with a list of questions that will all have a yes or no answer. Other types of questions can also be asked, but it will take some more in-depth work to interpret the sounds and shapes made in the burning grains.

Begin by lighting your charcoal briquettes. Your charcoal briquettes may or may not already have lighter fluid in them. If not, you might need to add some to get the coals started. I usually use a small portable grill and make a stack two layers thick by about five coals wide. It really depends on how long you're going to be asking questions! If you don't have a grill, you can also use a cast-iron skillet placed on top of two or three bricks for support, depending on the size of the skillet.

Once your coals are hot, throw on some red cedar to cleanse the space before you begin the divination ritual. While facing the hot coals, repeat this verbal charm three times: "Fire that lights the darkness, light my questioning mind. Speak to me in pops, sparks, and crackles. Let your words be true and easily understood. Blessed fire, light my path and I will give you beer to drink and bread to eat."

After you've repeated the charm, ask your first question aloud into the flames. Then, take a good-sized pinch of the grain mixture and toss it on the coals. Now, listen carefully to the sounds it makes and the way it burns. Continue in this same way with each of your questions. Here is a list of traditional Ozark symbols that can be derived from the fire, but allow yourself to make your own in-the-moment interpretations as well.

- **SUDDEN BURST OF FIRE:** Excitement from Fire

- **SLOW, STEADY LINE OF POPS AND CRACKLES:** Fire is thinking hard on the situation

- **LOTS OF QUICK POPS AND CRACKLES:** Affirmative answer to the question asked
- **SLOW SMOLDERING, LITTLE TO NO POPS OR CRACKLES:** Negative answer to the question asked

Practitioners who use this method of divination will also sometimes observe shapes that form in the burning grains or in the smoke, sometimes as answers to more open-ended questions. These symbols are usually similar to those read in tea leaves or candle wax. If you'd like to observe these signs, I recommend performing this ritual during the daytime rather than night. Here is a partial list, but again, try letting yourself see the symbols that you need to see in the moment.

- **ARROW:** Answer coming from the direction the arrow is pointing, or the answer can be found in that direction
- **BIRD:** Good luck; omen of travel
- **CLOUD:** Trouble overhead
- **CLOVER:** Very good luck
- **CROSS:** Delay in your work, trouble, or even death
- **HAMMER:** Challenges overcome
- **HORSESHOE:** Success and good luck
- **KNIFE:** Something needs to be cut from your life
- **MOON:** Happiness and success; dig deeper into what is hidden
- **MOUNTAIN:** An obstacle arises in your path
- **RING:** A contract, binding, or union
- **SNAKE:** Something is being hidden from you; using magic and cunning to discover the truth
- **SWORD:** Arguments and conflict up ahead
- **TREE:** Good luck, prosperity, fortune. Can also indicate an ancestor that wishes to reach out (family tree)
- **UMBRELLA:** Small annoyances and distractions

When you finish your questioning, don't forget to give the fire what you promised in the verbal charm! Place some pieces of bread on the coals and let them smolder.

Once they have been mostly burned up, pour a little beer over the coals and then let them burn out naturally in a safe place.

VARIATIONS: A variety of seeds, grains, and plants can be used in this ritual. The ones I've listed here are examples of ingredients that are easy to find and have been used by a wide range of magical practitioners. Some forego using grains at all and instead write their questions on squares of paper that they toss onto the coals, making sure to observe any shapes or symbols formed in the paper as it burns. One healer I met wrote her questions on larger squares of paper with all the letters capitalized and spaced out more than they normally would be. It looked strange to me, but I quickly realized the purpose as she placed the paper over a single layer of coals and watched which letters were immediately blacked out and which ones remained the longest. She made sure to quickly write down the letters that remained behind and then formed them into anagrams that she interpreted as answers to her questions.

BIBLE VERSE: You can replace the verbal charm in the original spell with Acts 2:17 and Acts 2:19. "In the last days it will be, God declares, that I will pour out my Spirit upon all flesh, and your sons and your daughters shall prophesy, and your young men shall see visions, and your old men shall dream dreams…And I will show portents in the heaven above and signs on the earth below, blood, and fire, and smoky mist."

NOTES: Divination by fire, smoke, and using a leaf on top of water were probably the three most widely used traditional Ozark methods, specifically for the diagnosis of magical illnesses. While there are Ozarkers who still use these methods today, they've mostly been replaced with tarot cards, oracle decks, runes, and pendulums. I'm happy to say that, in part because of my encouragement, there has been a recent resurgence of these older divination methods amongst younger practitioners.

RITUAL FOR DIVINATION USING SMOKE

MAGICAL TIMING: Full moon; Wednesday; Gemini

INGREDIENTS:

- Incense charcoal and burner, with metal tongs
- Knife
- Lighter or matches
- Plants for burning (see Spell section)
- Red cedar leaves and/or berries (*Juniperus virginiana*)

SPELL: As you can see from the ingredients list, there are many different plants you can use for this ritual. I recommended using specific plants for specific questions. Red cedar or common juniper, both the foliage and berries, are great all-purpose plants for this type of divination, but let yourself experiment with others on the following list as well as any other plants or resins you might prefer:

- **HORSEMINT LEAVES AND FLOWERS:** Questions about spirit entities, specifically non-ancestor entities, that might be bothering or haunting you
- **MUGWORT LEAVES:** Questions about general health, personal or for others; questions to help interpret dreams or trance visions
- **RED CEDAR LEAVES AND BERRIES OR COMMON JUNIPER:** Questions about ancestors and guiding spirits; questions about personal growth, healing, and cleansing
- **SWEETGUM RESIN:** Questions about things that are hidden; questions to reveal secrets or your enemy's identity
- **YARROW FLOWERS:** Questions regarding love and relationships

For this spell, it's better to work indoors to prevent any wind from interfering with the smoke. Likewise, make sure to turn off any overhead fans in the room where you are working this ritual. Petitions and questions are traditionally directed either at a divine power or at the smoke itself as its own entity. You can also ask any of your guiding spirits or ancestors to offer answers through symbols in the smoke.

Begin by lighting your charcoal by holding it in the flame from a lighter or matches, making sure to also use metal tongs as the coal will quickly get hot. Once lit, add a pinch of red cedar or juniper to cleanse the area in preparation for the reading. While it is smoking, cut through the smoke with the blade of your knife in the shape of a cross (up to down, left to right) three times. Then, clear any burnt debris off of the charcoal once it has stopped smoking.

Before adding your smoking plant, repeat this verbal charm three times, blowing across the coal after each recitation: "With my breath I give you life, little ember. Burn bright and let your smoke bring me an answer. Burn bright and guide my path. Burn bright and you will be blessed."

After repeating the charm, ask your first question and add a pinch of whichever plant or resin you will be using to the charcoal. For this divination ritual and all others,

I highly recommend that you have a notebook or some other recording device nearby to keep track of how the smoke responds throughout the ritual.

There are many ways of interpreting the smoke once you've asked a question, and you'll probably discover some of your own as you become more familiar with this practice. Here are some common smoke answers I've gathered from around the Ozarks:

- **SMOKE STILL AND RISING IN A CALM, STEADY LINE:** Listening and thinking; might not have an answer right now
- **SMOKE SPINS CLOCKWISE:** Affirmative answer to question asked
- **SMOKE SPINS COUNTERCLOCKWISE:** Negative answer to question asked
- **SMOKE RISES UP, THEN QUICKLY TAPERS OR BILLOWS OUT FROM THE CENTRAL STREAM:** Seek your answer from a higher power, guide, or ancestor
- **SMOKE MOVES IN RANDOM DIRECTIONS OR UP AND DOWN OR SIDE TO SIDE:** Someone or some entity is intentionally blocking the work; cleansing is needed

Once you're finished with your questioning, let the charcoal burn out naturally, then take any of the ash that remains and place it on the roots of an oak tree or any witch tree.

VARIATIONS: Here are some more smoke suggestions just to get you thinking about how you can incorporate your own favorite plants and resins into this ritual to make it a bit more personal. Suppose, for instance, that you're wanting to connect to some of your ancestors who were Catholic, Eastern Orthodox, Oriental Orthodox, or Muslim. For these religious groups, frankincense is still used on a daily basis in some holy sites as a way of not only cleansing the space from evil influences, but also to symbolically transform prayers into smoke that rises to heaven. Similarly, if you're from a Hindu, Sikh, or Buddhist background, or are connecting to ancestors who were from these cultures, try burning traditional incense from these areas, especially sandalwood. Maybe you've always loved the scent of jasmine and use it often in your rituals; perhaps pick up some dried jasmine flowers to use, or jasmine loose incense. The options are truly endless and are only limited by your own imagination.

The smoke for this form of divination doesn't always have to come from plant matter dropped on an incense charcoal. Several healers I met used smoke from tobacco pipes in their divination practices as well. They would draw smoke into their mouth, then first observe the smoke that trailed out of the bowl of the pipe before gently blowing the smoke from their mouth, observing next how this "cloud" was formed and moved in relation to the first.

Incense sticks and cones can also be used for this method. I've found, however, that the smoke trail is often small and hard to see with sticks and cones. The incense charcoal method makes for a much easier "cloud" to observe and interpret.

BIBLE VERSE: You can replace the verbal charm in the original spell with Psalm 141:1–2. "I call upon you, O Lord; come quickly to me; give ear to my voice when I call to you. Let my prayer be counted as incense before you, and the lifting up of my hands as an evening sacrifice."

NOTES: Remember that divination is an art and not everyone will connect with a specific method. That's why so many exist! Try out several different rituals to see which one fits with your own style and practice. You might discover that multiple methods call out to you, or you might find that none of them really resonate with your own work. Magic is always personal, so give yourself the freedom to explore and see what the Ozarks and your own heritage have to offer.

RITUAL FOR DIVINATION USING A SPICEBUSH LEAF

MAGICAL TIMING: Full moon; Monday (Cancer) or Thursday (Pisces)

INGREDIENTS:

- Bowl
- Knife
- Spicebush leaf, whole, fresh or dried (*Lindera benzoin*)
- Spring water

SPELL: This ritual again requires a room free from any moving air, or as free as you can get. This is a very sensitive method of divination, like using smoke in the last ritual, so it can easily be influenced by any ceiling fans, open windows, or even your own breath.

Begin by filling your bowl with water. Traditionally, Ozarkers would use spring water collected directly from the source. This isn't likely to be a possibility for most, so you can also use bottled spring water or even tap water if that's what you've got. Your bowl should be at least big enough to accommodate the spicebush leaf, allowing for some room around the leaf for movement; you really can't choose a bowl that's too big. I like to use a bowl that is white or light in color so I can easily observe the movement of the leaf.

Place your bowl of water on a flat surface like a tabletop. Before continuing, it's best to tell your spicebush leaf how it should answer. Determine which direction—clockwise and counterclockwise—will indicate a yes and which will be a no. Also, if you want to use the directional correspondences, sit facing the north during the ritual.

After you're situated, repeat this verbal charm three times: "Water stir, and water speak. Water let this leaf not sink. Let it float and do not fall. Let it answer when I call. Let it spin and answer fast. Answer all my questions, first to last." After each recitation, stir the water in a clockwise circle with the knife blade three times.

Suspend your spicebush leaf gently on top of the water so that it is floating as close to the center of the bowl as you can get. Ask your first question and observe how the leaf moves or spins, or what direction it might be floating in. If it sits motionless, move on to your next question. This method takes a great amount of patience and practice to perfect.

These are the traditional Ozark directional correspondences, so that if the leaf floats in a certain direction, you can determine what the leaf might be telling you. Remember, you should be sitting facing north if you want to use these correspondences.

- **NORTH:** Negative direction; land of "cold" creatures like frogs and toads; can indicate a "freezing" of the situation or a blockage that needs to be "thawed" or removed before proceeding

- **SOUTH:** Positive direction; the land of wealth, prosperity, and good luck; can indicate a fortuitous omen surrounding the question or situation

- **EAST:** Positive direction; land of healing, blessing, and cleansing; can indicate that higher-order spirits are attending to the situation or that a beneficial outcome will arrive quickly

- **WEST:** Negative direction; land of sickness and evil; connotations are that it is the opposite of the eastern correspondences; can indicate a cursed condition or that someone is working against you; can also indicate that a completely new method needs to be used to address the question or situation at hand

When you're finished asking your questions, take the bowl of water outside and pour it on the roots of an oak, a spicebush, or one of the witch trees. You can also use this blessed water on your houseplants or garden. Make sure to bury your spicebush leaf wherever you pour your water.

VARIATIONS: None

BIBLE VERSE: You can replace the verbal charm in the original spell with Genesis 1:1–3. "In the beginning when God created the heavens and the earth, the earth was a formless void and darkness covered the face of the deep, while a wind from God swept over the face of the waters. Then God said, 'Let there be light'; and there was light."

NOTES: Spicebush has a wide variety of uses, both medicinal and magical. Its name comes from the cinnamon scent of its leaves and bark, which has given rise to its other common name, spicewood. For many years, Ozark hillfolk used spicebush berries as a cinnamon or allspice substitute in their recipes as well as a flavoring agent for wild meats that were often very gamey. Tea made from the leaves and twigs of the plant has been used to help open the sinuses and drain out congestion. When brewed strong, the tea can be a febrifuge, meaning it will help you sweat out a fever. Because the plant is considered "warm," it can help aid in any "cold" conditions that might be found.

Magically, spicebush is also associated with cleansing and purification rites. Baths made from a combination of spicebush and sassafras leaves have been frequently used by Ozark healers to help cleanse sickness, the evil eye, and hexes. Healers who use the "sucking" method to magically remove illnesses and curses from their clients often make a "quid" or "chaw" of spicebush leaves in their mouth, which is said to help keep their spit purified during the rite and prevent anything they might be sucking and spitting out from traveling into their own bodies.

Like sassafras, spicebush has many associations with water, perhaps deriving from its preferred environment in the shadow of the thick canopy overhead, growing alongside creeks and rivers. It's interesting to note that the two plants are in the same family, *Lauraceae*, which is perhaps why hillfolk would have noted similarities between the plants and thereby used them in similar ways. Because of their watery associations, there is a strict taboo never to burn any part of the sassafras or spicebush. Wood from both plants is said to pop and spark heavily when burned, leading to the risk of cabin fires.

A HOLE STONE FOR THE SECOND SIGHT

MAGICAL TIMING: New moon to full moon; Thursday; Pisces

INGREDIENTS:

- Hole stone
- 12 "impossible" ingredients:
  1. A five-leaf clover
  2. Rain collected on May Day
  3. Leaves from a red cedar growing out of solid rock
  4. A clump of moss that's never touched the ground
  5. Water flowing to the east
  6. Three mistletoe leaves collected on the Winter Solstice
  7. Leaves from a holly growing out of a sycamore tree
  8. An apple growing on an oak tree (oak gall)
  9. Spring water that's never seen the sun
  10. Snow collected on Christmas Day
  11. Hound's tongue, but not the animal, leaves and flowers (*Andersonglossum virginianum*)
  12. Soot from seven chimneys

- Large bowl or bucket

SPELL: This ritual is for creating a hole stone with the intended purpose of being able to look through the hole and peer into the otherworld of spirits, ghosts, and the Little People. Charms like these have been used in particular by healers to be able to magically see any illnesses or curses that might be hiding inside of their clients. This powerful tool is made even stronger when used by someone who already has an inborn connection to magic. You might find the ingredients of this ritual difficult to acquire, hence their label of "impossible," but great power often demands great sacrifice. None of these items are truly impossible to find, although their identity might be hidden behind a riddle.

Once all of your ingredients have been assembled, take and combine all the liquids that appear on the ingredients list in a bowl. You can also add regular spring water or even tap water to help fill the container if you only collected small amounts of the "impossible" liquids. Next, add all of the rest of your ingredients to the bowl. Finally, drop in your hole stone. Recite this verbal charm three times, blowing across the water after each recitation: "From the mountain above to the valley below. From rocky cliffs, hills, and hollers. From rivers, creeks, and hidden springs. From deep caverns below my feet. Up from tree and rock! Up from earth! Out of stump, sprout, and sprig! I gather all of this power here. Twelve gifts I give for the second sight."

Leave your stone in the water for all days of the waxing moon. Every day, recite the verbal charm three times along with the three breaths. At midnight on the full moon, preferably in Pisces, repeat your verbal charm and the blowing ritual three more times, then take the hole stone out of the water.

Properly disposing of the water and your twelve "impossible" ingredients is very important. You can bury it all in the ground; if you have an outdoor shrine or workspace, you can actually bury it there for added power. You can throw it into a river or creek that flows to the east. You can also pour it across the mouth of a cave so that the water touches both the light outside and the dark inside. I don't recommend using the water as a pour-over bath as its power can easily overwhelm and, according to folk belief, cause uncontrollable visions of the otherworld.

VARIATIONS: No substitutions can be made for the items and ingredients in this ritual. There are many other similarly "impossible" ingredients and rituals all aimed at acquiring power or some magical gift / tool. Some I've encountered have involved many more ingredients and steps than this one, so consider yourself fortunate. One old adage that I might pass along to you: the journey is sometimes more important and meaningful than the destination. Don't get too bogged down in the finer details of the spell and its ingredients list. Many of the items are left open to interpretation, and as I've found, the otherworld often rewards those who are cunning.

BIBLE VERSE: None

NOTES: In addition to the many other benefits of the hole stone, it is also associated with the "second sight," sometimes just called "the sight" by Ozarkers. This ability can manifest in a couple different ways. First, it could be a sort of prognostication, or the ability to foresee future events before they occur. It can also refer to the ability to see, or sense, spirits of the dead as well as otherworldly beings like angels, Little People, etc. For some, the sight encompasses both of these areas.

While the sight is generally considered to be an inborn gift, there are tales about hillfolk being gifted the power, or finding the power through interactions with magical tools like the hole stone. Hole stones as well as hole roots are seen as natural openings or doorways into the magical otherworld. For this reason, it's often said that looking through the hole in a hole stone or root will let a person see the Little People and other spirits, especially if they already have an inborn magical gift.

This power does come with a warning, though, that looking through the hole stone too much can corrupt your own vision. In some tales, a person can go blind in that eye as a result of this habit. In other stories, the person is cursed with one eye that always sees into the otherworld, no doubt leading to a very disorienting sense of perception.

MAKING A DOWSING ROD

MAGICAL TIMING: New moon to full moon; Gemini

INGREDIENTS:

- Camphor essential oil
- Cloth, white, at least 3-feet square, or a white blanket
- Incense charcoal and burner, with metal tongs
- Lighter or matches
- Offering mixture for spirits: equal parts oats, whole barley, and cornmeal
- Olive oil
- Red cedar leaves, dried or fresh (*Juniperus virginiana*)
- Silver item, preferably a ring or necklace
- Witch hazel branch (*Hamamelis virginiana*), Y-shaped

SPELL: Please note that there are many different rituals for making dowsing rods. This is just one that I was given, and it's always resonated with my own practice. Some successful dowsers haven't used any rituals in their craft and simply choose a properly shaped branch seemingly at random, or they base their selection simply on how long the branch is and how pliable it is when held in the hands.

The first part of this ritual involves finding the proper witch hazel branch. In this case, it should be a Y shape first and foremost. It should be anywhere from two to two-and-a-half feet long in total, with the tips of the Y branches being at least nine to twelve inches apart from each other. Having them too close will interfere with the movement of the rod. The length of the individual Y branches themselves varies, but they should be long enough for you to hold each side loosely in your hands, as in this picture:

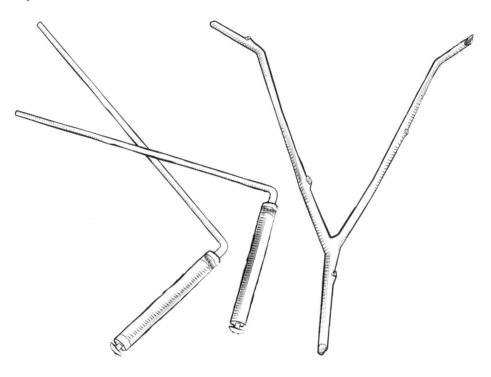

Once you've found a proper rod, you will want to petition the plant by sprinkling your offering mixture at its roots in a clockwise circle while repeating this prayer: "Witch hazel, I need your power, I need your branch. Witch hazel, I give you this food as payment. Witch hazel, I break one branch, but let a hundred more grow to replace it."

When you've finished the prayer and given your offerings, break—don't cut—off the branch. (Some dowsers do cut their branches, but the practitioner who gave me this specific ritual was very clear that no metal should come into contact with the rod.) Once the branch is broken from the main bush, you can clean off any leaves or smaller branches and even trim down the branches that form the Y shape, all by hand, of course. Once you're finished, take your rod back home to bless it.

Beginning on the new moon, after sundown, smoke your dowsing rod with red cedar leaves or common juniper. Then, place your silver item so that it's constantly touching the rod. I suggest a silver ring that you can slide over one of the branches, or a silver chain you can wrap around the rod. Recite this verbal charm while you wrap your rod (and the silver item) in a piece of white cloth or a white blanket: "Little Hazel, go to sleep. Little Hazel, go to bed. Tomorrow we'll have work to do, but for now, dream, little Hazel, dream." This was called "putting the rod to bed" by my informant.

Once your rod is wrapped up, place it in a safe spot to "sleep." You'll repeat the smoking, wrapping in cloth, and the verbal charm every night until the next full moon, preferably in Gemini.

On the full moon, remove the silver item from your dowsing rod. Then wash the branch in clean water. After that, dry off the branch. Finally, smoke the branch with red cedar one more time. Anoint the three tips of the Y shape with an oil made from twelve drops of camphor essential oil mixed with a cup of olive oil. Save this mixture to anoint the tips again every new and full moon.

VARIATIONS:

- While witch hazel is the most common wood used to make dowsing rods in the Ozarks, other trees are also traditional if they are easier to acquire in your area. These include the willow (*Salix* spp.) and peach tree. In Europe, the hazel (*Corylus* spp.) is commonly used for dowsing rods, so these branches are also suitable.

- You can also use the original ritual to bless dowsing rods made of any material. The ritual is good for L-shaped rods also. Just leave out the ritual branch gathering in the beginning.

BIBLE VERSE: None

NOTES: Traditional dowsers are still consulted to this day, usually to find underground water for digging wells. But there are other types of dowsers as well, including those who can find hidden ore deposits under the ground, natural gas, caves, buried treasure, and even the location where dead bodies are buried. There have been many studies into the actual efficacy of the dowser's practice, and many results have shown that these gifted individuals are correct as frequently as anyone else would be just taking a wild guess. I myself still believe in the art, having met many gifted dowsers whose power was more than convincing to me that something magical is indeed present in the practice. True dowsers tend to be very secretive people, though, and wouldn't likely agree to a test of their ability in the first place.

Conclusion

I'VE BEEN VERY FORTUNATE IN my travels across the Ozark region to be able to collect so many rituals, remedies, and recipes from both traditional and what I like to call "neotraditional" practitioners. I spend the majority of my time these days amongst the neotraditional practitioners, and it's where my own work falls. The neotraditionalists take the core of Ozark folk belief and expand it to include a whole host of other ancestral practices and traditions that wouldn't have been known or accepted by the more conservative Ozarkers of the past. In reality, many of these so-called new traditions are actually ancient beliefs and practices, just brought forward into a more modern context. Most Ozark practices, even those in the more traditional school, have evolved from these individual ancient puzzle pieces. Through the passing down from practitioner to practitioner, however, the original contexts of many of these pieces have been lost. Reconnecting to that original, ancestral context behind folk practices and beliefs is so important to many of the neotraditional practitioners, myself included, and there are many ways we've been able to help evolve Ozark traditions by rediscovering treasure troves of culture buried by our ancestors.

RECLAIMING IDENTITIES

One example of this evolution is found in the reclamation movements within various traditional witchcraft systems, in particular those of European origin. Many of these systems have become increasingly popular over the past few years but have been around since ancient days. Individual practitioners within these systems look for traditions and practices beyond the borders of their colonized countries, back to the homelands of their ancestors. This movement has been particularly popular here in the United States, where so many of us have such fragmented cultural identities. The temptation within magical and spiritual communities has always been to fill in the gaps within our own broken heritage with pieces we can find, or often buy, from other cultures. As is often the case, these pieces are usually highly commercialized and taken entirely out of context. Indigenous people around the world have been the most damaged by this grab-bag approach to spiritual traditions. Reclamation systems arose in part as a response to this exact mentality, in particular amongst mostly white practitioners from a pan-European background. The idea being that rather than taking from already marginalized and at-risk cultures, there is such a wealth of information from within their own ancestral backgrounds just waiting to be reinvigorated.

Identity can be a tricky thing. I'll use myself as an example. For a long time, I've connected to my Ozark heritage, knowing full well that Ozark culture is itself a complicated subject, being an amalgam of Old and New World traditions, often with very blurred lines in between. I'm also my family's genealogist and I've spent many, many hours tracing my family tree back to its European roots. As with many Americans, that's a complicated issue as well. How should I reconnect to and practice my own ancestral traditions when my ancestors came from so many diverse places across Europe including England, Scotland, Cornwall, Wales, Ireland, France, Germany, Norway, Sweden, and Finland? And this is only going back to the 1600s. Who knows what sort of migrations and changes are represented in my blood? And how far does one go back in time to look for culture? All the way to the Indo-European herders and hunters? Or should it be even farther back than that? It's enough to make your head spin, and in the case of many practitioners I've met, they lose all hope of connecting to their ancestral traditions altogether.

EVER-EVOLVING TRADITIONS

I walk a much calmer road these days. I recognize that Ozark traditions are always going to be a complicated mixture of many different parts. I also recognize that the very word *tradition* itself is a bit meaningless, at least in the way most people use it today. I don't know how many times I've talked to Ozarkers who have angrily denounced the forward movement of time, choosing instead to latch on to nostalgic images of the "good ol' days." Others have held more depressing sentiments like "All our traditions are gone" or "Ozark traditions are dead." Old-timers can often be very dramatic when it comes to such proclamations. I do have to admit, though, they are correct when it comes to the culture portrayed by folklorists like Vance Randolph back in the 1930s and '40s. For the most part, the traditions he and others recorded really aren't around anymore. Small pockets of the "old Ozarks" might be found in isolated rural communities, but glimpses of that bygone era are mostly relegated to campfire stories and cultural reenactments. But before you become morose, I'd like to argue that the culture Randolph created in his works (as well as others aiming at a mostly non-Ozark audience) never really existed in the way he portrayed it anyway.

This is an unpopular opinion amongst some historians and has gotten me into trouble in the past. These types will cite Ozarkers as fierce protectors of their insular cultures against all outside influences. They will talk about how when electricity first came to many of the rural areas, it didn't last long as hillfolk kept stripping the wires off all the poles for their own uses. They'll talk about the battles, both ideological and physical, between hillfolk and the non-Ozark farmers who built up towns in the fertile valley areas and brought in dangerous "foreign" medicines, amongst other things. All of this is indeed a part of our past, but certainly not unique to Ozark people. Hillfolk didn't suddenly start being isolated and protective of their culture when they moved to these mountains.

Despite protests from a few historians, I still hold to my original opinion: that Ozark hillfolk have always been willing to incorporate outside traditions into their own canon, as well as evolve their own traditions to survive the changing times. At the most basic, practical level, this ever-evolving culture is a way to ensure survival of the family, and hillfolk have always had survival at the crux of all their traditions and practices.

One of the finest pieces of advice given to me by an Ozark healer were these simple words: "If it works, it works." Just look at the spells contained in this book as a small example of this. Here we have a mixture of European, Indigenous, and homegrown Ozark elements all coming together to make something that works. If hillfolk had been as averse to outside influences as presented by many folklorists and historians, the majority of our traditions would never have existed. The same can be said for all of our traditions all the way back through time. Tradition is never static. It evolves as people evolve, and those traditions that can't move forward with the times get left behind.

FILLING IN THE GAPS

It's long been my opinion that we practitioners base entirely too much of our own practice and connection to culture upon what folklorists and historians have left to us. This is especially true for cultures like my own, where there is already so little recorded information that whatever we do find written in the folk accounts we take as the complete, unchangeable truth. Traditions of Ozark folk magic and healing can often differ drastically from family to family. Practices that are vital to one healer might seem like something completely unnecessary to another. As I've often said, there are as many different practices as there are practitioners in the Ozarks. Historically, these practices were closely guarded secrets, passed down only by word of mouth and usually through family lines alone, so it's not surprising to say that the folklorists, despite their large collections of recorded material, weren't able to encounter *everything* hillfolk had to offer. In many cases, this lack of verifying information from the folklorists left huge gaps in our folk knowledge. For some, the gaps are good reminders of the importance of collecting traditional knowledge before it's too late. For others, they can be an utterly frustrating stumbling block along the path.

This frustration often leads to the temptation to fill in these gaps with things we've encountered from other traditions around us. Sometimes the temptation might be to take certain practices or traditions from cultures we've deemed more "spiritual" than our own. Indigenous people around the world have constantly had to live with this stereotype and likewise have had a never-ending battle against the appropriation of their traditions. This isn't to say that looking to outside cultures to fill in the missing pieces within our own is entirely bad; it isn't. I recommend to my own students that where those gaps appear, they should look to their own ancestry as a guide. This is something I myself practice.

We have to remember that Ozark culture didn't just appear out of nowhere; it's an amalgam of many different traditions, beliefs, and practices. By tracing these practices back to their original sources, we can sometimes dig up enough context and information to re-create something within our own Ozark identity. I'll give one example from my own life.

In my own work as a witch and healer, I often work with trance in order to access parts of my own power not normally available in ordinary time and space. The more traditional Ozark practitioners and healers have had very little to say about the subject of trance, especially trances that utilize certain plants as allies. The most I've ever gotten out of anyone was an older lady who said she knew a "witch woman" when she was a kid who used "some kind of nightshade plant" that she gathered in the woods to go into a trance. Other stories follow a very similar path. This isn't to say that Ozark practitioners never historically worked with trance or any specific trance-inducing plant species—they most certainly did. There is a whole trove of tall tales about witches who do this very thing and while these stories are often very fanciful, many have a core of truth hidden beneath the fantasy.

With this lack of Ozark-specific traditional knowledge, I could have either given up completely or avoided practicing my craft until I had the information I was looking for. I chose to take a different route and instead looked backward through my own ancestry to Europe, specifically Indigenous British (i.e., Cornish, Welsh, etc.), German, and Scandinavian sources to fill in this gap within my own Ozark heritage. What I found was an abundance of information about traditional plant concoctions made from various trance-inducing plants, including the famous "flying ointments" that appear in witch accounts across medieval Europe.

More than just discovering practices from my own ancestry that I could incorporate into my work, I caught a glimpse of traditions that might very well have inspired the fragments I was collecting several hundred years later across the world. Perhaps the nightshade plant mentioned by several Ozark old-timers was actually one of these Old World plants used in the famous flying ointments. We might never have complete confirmation of this, at least not in a way that would satisfy the folklorist or historian. As practitioners, though, connecting to this process of looking back to our own ancestors, wherever they were from, isn't just a practical tool but can become an actual *practice* in and of itself, the practice of honoring our blood and work.

YOUR EVER-GROWING SPELL BOOK

This work isn't just my own. Nor does it belong to Ozark people alone. As you read through my spells and rituals, you might have found the magic pumping through your own veins. You might have thought to yourself how similar our practices really are, or how a tradition from the Ozark hills and hollers seems somehow so familiar to you. The magic at the heart of my own practice is the same that's at the heart of yours as well.

You're now a part of this story, if you choose to be. Spells have a way of taking on their own lives, if we let them. They can grow, expand, and evolve outward into that infinite creative darkness that surrounds our souls. Where gaps and missing pieces might appear in my spells, think about how you can bring some of your own cultural traditions and practices into the work. In this way, we can create an ever-growing spell book together.

Bibliography

Banks, William H. *Plants of the Cherokee: Medicinal, Edible, and Useful Plants of the Eastern Cherokee Indians*. Gatlinburg, TN: Great Smoky Mountains Association, 2004.

Blevins, Brooks. *Arkansas/Arkansaw: How Bear Hunters, Hillbillies, and Good Ol' Boys Defined a State*. Fayetteville, AR: University of Arkansas Press, 2011.

———. *Hill Folks: A History of Arkansas Ozarkers and Their Image*. Chapel Hill, NC: University of North Carolina Press, 2002.

———. *A History of the Ozarks, Volume 1: The Old Ozarks*. Urbana, IL: University of Illinois Press, 2018.

———. *A History of the Ozarks, Volume 2: The Conflicted Ozarks*. Urbana, IL: University of Illinois Press, 2019.

Brinker, Francis. *Herbal Contraindications and Drug Interactions: Plus Herbal Adjuncts with Medicines*. 4th ed. Sandy, OR: Eclectic Medical Publications, 2010.

Easley, Thomas, and Steven Horne. *The Modern Herbal Dispensatory: A Medicine-Making Guide*. Berkeley, CA: North Atlantic Books, 2016.

Frazer, James George. *The Golden Bough*. New York: Dover Publications, 2019.

Grieve, M. *A Modern Herbal: The Medicinal, Culinary, Cosmetic, and Economic Properties, Cultivation and Folklore of Herbs, Grasses, Fungi, Shrubs, and Trees with All Their Modern Scientific Uses*. London: Tiger Books International, 1998.

Mooney, James. *James Mooney's History, Myths, and Sacred Formulas of the Cherokees*. Fairview, NC: Bright Mountain Books, 1992.

Parler, Mary Celestia. *Mary Celestia Parler Folklore Collection*. 1950.

———. *Folk Beliefs from Arkansas*. Self-published, 1962.

Randolph, Vance. "Nakedness in Ozark Folk Belief." *The Journal of American Folklore* 66, no. 262 (October 1953): 333–39. https://doi.org/10.2307/536729.

———. *Ozark Magic and Folklore*. New York: Dover Publications, 2003.

Rayburn, Otto Ernest. Papers. Special Collections Department, University of Arkansas Libraries.

———. "Bloodstoppers in the Ozarks." *Midwest Folklore* 4, no. 4 (1954): 213–15. https://www.jstor.org/stable/4317482.

———. "The 'Granny-Woman' in the Ozarks." *Midwest Folklore* 9, no. 3 (1959): 145–48. https://www.jstor.org/stable/4317804.

———. *Ozark Country*. New York: Duell, Sloan & Pearce, 1960.

TO WRITE TO THE AUTHOR

If you wish to contact the author or would like more information about this book, please write to the author in care of Llewellyn Worldwide Ltd. and we will forward your request. Both the author and publisher appreciate hearing from you and learning of your enjoyment of this book and how it has helped you. Llewellyn Worldwide Ltd. cannot guarantee that every letter written to the author can be answered, but all will be forwarded. Please write to:

Brandon Weston
⅟ Llewellyn Worldwide
2143 Wooddale Drive
Woodbury, MN 55125-2989

Please enclose a self-addressed stamped envelope for reply,
or $1.00 to cover costs. If outside the U.S.A., enclose
an international postal reply coupon.

Many of Llewellyn's authors have websites with additional information and resources. For more information, please visit our website at http://www.llewellyn.com.

NOTES